173 Hour

NEELESH MISRA is a
Associated Press in
Lucknow in 1973 a:
Lucknow. He started writing in English and
Hindi in 1989 in Lucknow, before taking up
journalism as a career. He has covered some of the
biggest news stories in India over the last five
years, including the Kargil war, the cyclone in
Orissa, earthquakes and floods, India's nuclear
tests and the elections, the Kashmir insurgency, a
mid-air jet crash and a series of political scandals.
Misra also has other interests — he has written
and acted in plays, and writes and sings in Hindi.

173 Hours in Captivity

THE HIJACKING OF IC 814

Neelesh Misra

HarperCollins *Publishers* India

HarperCollins *Publishers* India Pvt Ltd
7/16 Ansari Road, Daryaganj, New Delhi 110 002

Published 2000 by
HarperCollins *Publishers* India

ISBN 81-7223-394-9

Typeset in Palatino by
Nikita Overseas Pvt Ltd
19-A, Ansari Road, Daryaganj
New Delhi 110 002

Printed in India by
Gopsons Papers Ltd
A-14, Sector 60
Noida 201 301

To
my parents
and to the parents
of Ripan Katyal,
who never came back

Contents

Contents

Acknowledgements

This book was written by a lot of people. My thanks to the passengers and the crew of Flight IC 814 for their help, time, interviews and ideas. My colleagues pitched in with their extremely valuable comments, suggestions and all possible help. I would specially like to thank Kathy Gannon, the untiring correspondent of Associated Press in Islamabad, Donna Bryson in Cairo, Faiza Ambah and Tarek Issawi in Dubai, Sherwin Crasto and Ramola Talwar Badam in Mumbai and Binaj Gurubacharya in Kathmandu.

A big thank you to my bureau chief Arthur Max, news editor Laurinda Keys and my colleagues in the New Delhi bureau for their help and encouragement. Journalist and friend Arun Joshi in Jammu provided crucial help in information gathering.

Thanks to Gaurav Arya, a friend and the right man to ask about everything from grenades to RDX to radio sets.

Several other news sources and well-wishers will remain anonymous, but let me mention that I am very grateful for their help and encouragement.

Thanks to Renuka Chatterjee and Amit Agarwal at HarperCollins for their patience and for having faith in this first-time author, and to friend and trusted troubleshooter Vincent Van Ross for all his help.

PROLOGUE

A messianic mullah in a Jammu jail ... and at Kathmandu airport, a wad of currency notes, a bag of weapons and a plate of chicken ... and a delayed flight

T he man in the bushy black beard caressed his sacred rosary with his thick fingers and sat motionless as the fading afternoon sunlight filtered into his room — like a capricious grandfather whose silence is feared more than his words. He arched his eyebrows and glided his eyes from right to left, back and forth, from behind the rectangular metallic frame of his spectacles as he zigzagged down the pages of a yellowing book of Koranic teachings in Urdu.

But Maulana Masood Azhar was no grandfather. He was a portly Pakistani bachelor who prayed five times a day, slept clutching his rosary with his fingers, spoke little, read a lot, clung to his small transistor radio and wore a flowing shalwar kameez.

And he was in jail.

It was 24 December 1999, the last Christmas Eve of the twentieth century, but in barrack number nine at the fort-like Kot Bhalwal prison in the northern Indian city of Jammu, the raucous festivity sweeping across the rest of the world seemed so many light years away.

Inside the single-storeyed yellow-washed building encircled by barbed wire, the man behind the solid iron bars had a face masked in a steely calm and eyes that sparkled with a glint that seemed to say: "I know all."

Keeping in proportion with the rest of Azhar's broad-shouldered, muscle-fattened hulk, the nose was large and gently arched downwards, the cheeks were puffed, and shallow furrows ran across his forehead. Once in a rare while, he looked up and a gentle wry smile showed up on the thickset lips almost hidden beneath the dense moustaches and flowing beard.

Azhar meant different things to different people.

For India's military, he was the ruthless, emotionless face of terror, the kind of man who inspired campaigns of bombings, ambushes and guerilla warfare that sapped the energies of Kashmir's people, army and the government in a never-ending insurgency. He was among those seemingly invincible fountainheads of terror whose inspiration churned out thousands of Islamic zealots.

Azhar was among the big trophies for India's soldiers in a festering war against Islamic guerillas: he was the cunning schemer, the king of propaganda, the master financier — something of a Machiavelli, Goebbels and Midas all rolled into one rotund package.

For thousands of Islamic guerillas fighting a tiring war against India's security forces in Kashmir for ten years now, Azhar was Allah's warrior, the wise and well-connected guru who showed the way in their jehad or holy war against India, the finance honcho who gave them the money that bought them bread and arms. He was the leader of the Harkat-ul Mujahideen, one of the frenzied terrorist outfits carrying out a no-holds-barred campaign against Indian rule in Kashmir. Azhar was too precious for both sides. A majority of the thirteen barracks in the Kot Bhalwal prison were occupied by about twenty-five prisoners, most of whom deeply revered Azhar. He was so respected that the prison authorities gave him a relatively spacious cell, though he had to share it with others. He spoke rarely with the others, instead making contact with the outside world through an Urdu newspaper which a sentry delivered to him each morning, and on his transistor radio on which news bulletins from several regional stations crackled every once in a while.

Nearly four months ago, in September 1999, the same radio transistor had brought Azhar news that had completely shattered him — Sajjad Khan, popularly known among the militants' ranks as Sajjad Afghani, his beloved comrade, fellow prison inmate and formerly the supreme commander of the Harkat-ul Ansar in the Kashmir valley, was dead. Within months, it would prove to be a costly death for India.

According to Indian officials, Azhar presided over a daring jailbreak plan in which Afghani and terrorist leader Nasarullah Langriyal led their inmate accomplices in digging a 23-feet tunnel leading out of the prison. Jail officials found out, when they were just a few feet short of freedom, and stormed the barracks. Several inmates pelted stones at policemen. Afghani was killed in a baton charge and riot in which several policemen were also wounded.

Critics of the police, however, said that Afghani had been tortured to death during investigation after the jailbreak plan was busted.

Afghani's death shook up Azhar. He wrote a long letter to Afghani's parents nearly three months after his death — a few weeks before that 24 December evening:

"Revered and fortunate parents of my dearest brother Commander Hafiz Sajjad Khan Shahid,

"Assalaamu'alaikum wa Rahimahullahu wa barkatohu!

"Two months and twenty days have gone by since the shahada (martyrdom) of my beloved brother. During this time I often thought of writing a letter to you but I could not find the courage to do so. My thoughts and my pen failed me.

"Both of us were arrested together and passed the next five years and four months in the same prison. There developed a mental and spiritual affinity between us which the coming calamities could not break. Together we faced the never-ending hardships of prison life, and shared each other's joys and sorrows, fears and apprehensions. Then suddenly he went away ... to become the guest of Allah Ta'ala.

"I doubt if anyone can understand how traumatic his separation from me was. No one knows what I went through.

"On the day of his shahada, just before the Asr (late afternoon) prayers I was lying on the bed, my heart heavy with sorrow. None of us had been told about his shahada at that time. All we knew was that he was in a very bad state due to the torture of the mushrikeen (renegades). I seem to have dozed off. Very clearly I saw him sitting on my bed with his hand upon my knee. 'I have become a shaheed (martyr). I have come to ask your forgiveness. And please hurry up for I have to go up.'

"Wide awake, now I hurried to the radio and started tuning in to different stations. Nearly an hour later the local Jammu Radio Station announced his shahada."

Afghani's death spurred a wave of anger among the guerilla groups, and they planned revenge. By New Year's Eve, the death was to become a flash point in the battle of Islamic guerillas against Indian forces, the provocation for a stunning strike in which Azhar would be set free.

But he lived a comfortable prison life even while he was there. Although he shared a barrack with other prisoners, he was special. He commanded the respect of the prisoners as well as the prison staff. He played the all-knowing guru and faith healer to fellow inmates and several guards.

Many of Azhar's admirers came to him to have their body aches cured with a seemingly magical therapy under which Azhar rubbed his hand across their foreheads or other hurting parts of the body and blew his warm breath softly as he circled his thick lips.

When he went to the court for his trial, he walked like a benevolent king, gently getting off the police van as he looked around at the crowds of his supporters that jostled and pushed at police barricades. Dozens of people stretched out their hands as Azhar handed out talismans for luck to his admirers.

Those seeking his blessings often included police officials themselves.

Azhar was held in awe by most people who knew about him. He was a powerful orator, believed to be fluent in more than a dozen languages. For the hordes of Islamic militants desperate and restless inside the high-security prison, he was the "ideas man." After his arrest, he had often told prison officials they would not be able to hold him for long.

He was charged under India's tough anti-terrorist law which has mostly meant years of tortuous waiting for the prisoner in the labyrinths of the country's courts — often without trial. He was himself hungry for freedom.

He wrote to Afghani's parents:

"This year in the month of Ramazan all of us had sincerely, earnestly prayed for shahada, or for release from jail. Sajjad's prayers have been granted while the rest of us are waiting. Who will be the one to lie next to Sajjad in the Jammu graveyard, no one knows. If I become the lucky one then I ask you to pray for me too."

Azhar did not become "the lucky one."

For the thousands of Muslim youths getting sucked into armed jehads against a string of governments across the world, Azhar was an icon, a legend, a man who rose swiftly from being an ordinary student at a Koranic school to become one of the most powerful Islamic separatist leaders today.

Azhar was born to school headmaster Allah Baksh Sabir and Pukia Biwi on 10 July 1968. In his interrogation by Indian investigators in December 1994, he said he did not remember his date of birth.

Azhar lived on a poultry farm in Kaunsar Colony in the Pakistani town of Bahawalpur with his five brothers and six sisters. He dropped out of school in 1979 when he was in the eighth grade, and then, on an uncle's insistence, was sent to an Islamic seminary called the Jamia Aloom Islamia Banwari Town Madrassa, in Karachi. Ten years later, in April 1989, he completed a degree course equivalent to a masters, and seminary authorities were so impressed with his intellect that he was appointed a teacher. Azhar refused a salary "for the cause of Islamisation."

The school was a hub of radicals from different Islamic countries from Africa to South-east Asia who learnt how to wage war against infidels and, in a few years, would look up to heroes like Osama Bin Laden and Azhar himself for inspiration.

In April 1989, Azhar came in touch with top leaders of the Harkat-ul Mujahideen, including the outfit's chief, Maulana Fazal-ur-Rehman Khalili, who invited him to a weapons' training camp in Yawar Khost in Afghanistan to fight Russian troops in that country. Azhar reached there with twenty other youths in a Toyota van.

Khost was the most important of four such training camps in Afghanistan, believed to have been planned and constructed by Osama Bin Laden, then a civil engineer, with the backing of the United States government, which was organising an Afghan rebellion against the Russian troops. Thousands of Islamic radicals engaged in guerilla warfare around the world are alumni of the Khost camp.

Azhar signed up for a tough armed training course that involved physical training, and handling of Kalashnikov rifles and medium machine guns — but it soon became clear that the portly man would be better off behind a desk than a machine gun.

"Since I was obese, I was not doing well in the training and Fazal-ur-Rehman, the chief of the outfit, debarred me from further training and directed me to return to Karachi," Azhar told his investigators.

The man who failed as a fighter returned to the seminary, where his pupils included young boys from South Africa, Indonesia, Malaysia, Zambia, the United Arab Emirates and Somalia. He was on his way to becoming someone more powerful — the strategist.

But first, he became a journalist. He was put in charge of the *Sada-e-Mujahed*, a new twenty-four-page monthly journal that was circulated free at religious gatherings.

Azhar made a swift climb up the hierarchy of the Harkat-ul Mujahideen. By 1993, he was senior enough to be given the task of streamlining the outfit's operations in Kashmir, and to play the pivotal role in bringing together three rival militant groups which merged to form the pro-Pakistan Harkat-ul Ansar. The outfit would become the main troublemaker for the Indian Army in Kashmir.

Azhar departed for India, arriving on 29 January 1994 via Bangladesh, travelling under an assumed name and a fake Portuguese passport. For a few days, Masood Azhar was transformed into Wali Adam Issa of Lisbon.

Eleven days later, on 9 February, he had reached his destination, Srinagar. A day later, he held what could be called a summit meeting of the top leaders of three terrorist groups which were still operating separately in Kashmir though they had formally merged in Pakistan — the Harkat-ul Mujahideen, the Harkat-ul Jehad-e-Islami and the Jamait-ul Mujahideen.

If the hierarchy of the Harkat-ul Ansar was a corporate ladder, Azhar had long become a senior executive. His career was soaring.

But then, he ran into a few moments of bad luck.

At about 10 a.m. on 11 February 1994, as Azhar, Sajjad Afghani and another associate drove back from the meeting, they were confronted by a patrol of the paramilitary Border Security Force. The third man in the Ambassador car fired, the soldiers fired back, and ultimately Azhar and Afghani were arrested.

Since his arrest, Azhar had been kept in this expansive prison with dirty cream walls spanning across 12.5 acres, on the outskirts of Jammu. As on other days, it was milling with guards on 24 December 1999, fortified by stone walls fifteen feet high.

Azhar sat in his prison cell completely engrossed in his book, his fingers gently rubbing the rosary beads in a mechanical action, his shoulders slightly hunched, his eyes straining over the text.

Seven mornings later, he would break free of those walls.

Hundreds of miles away to the east in the Nepalese capital of Kathmandu, events were revolving around a wad of currency notes, a handbag with weapons and a plate of gravy-dipped chicken.

The line was getting longer at the Indian Airlines check-in counter at the Tribhuvan International Airport, which has a red brick building nestling between mountains. Two clerks mechanically printed out boarding cards, luggage trolleys jammed the lounge, and passengers stood grumbling about how slowly the line was moving.

The Indian Airlines flight IC 814 was delayed by more than three hours.

Even at the best of times, the Tribhuvan International Airport is a free-for-all. Today was no different. One of the two X-ray machines was not working. Several passengers had kept their bags on the steel rollers which refused to move. Then, with a little spurt, the luggage was pushed between the shredded leather curtains where it was to be examined. Nothing of the sort happened. Finally a policeman in a blue uniform pulled out the bags — and nonetheless pasted the tag: "Security Checked."

Two of these bags belonged to Ibrahim Athar — a reddish golf bag full of explosives, and a bigger blue and white bag with a lot of weapons.

Athar was a short, bespectacled man, apparently in his late thirties, with broad shoulders and a gently protruding belly. He wore gold-rimmed spectacles with photo-chromatic glasses that settled nicely on his round face. Athar happened to be the younger brother of Masood Azhar, the portly guru in Jammu prison, and he lived in Bahawalpur in the same house as the rest of the family.

After the bags got the security stickers and went through the conveyor belt, Athar walked to the phones near the exit, and made two calls. One of them was to Bombay. *"Samaan chalaa gaya hai"* (The luggage is through), he said. Then he called a local hotel where four of his associates were sitting ready and packed, waiting for his go-ahead. He told them he had checked in, and asked them to come. Athar then walked to the long line at the counter and checked in.

Within a short while, the four other men drove up to the airport and checked in separately. One of them, Sunny Ahmed Qazi, also called Muhammad Mansoor, clutched four tickets and got four boarding cards, all suprisingly listed under his name. Three of them were for the economy class, the fourth for the business class. He asked for separate seats, spread across the aircraft from the front to the rear.

Five men who were travelling together would sit on separate seats inside the plane, and it would take a while to figure out why: in a meticulously planned operation, they were about to hijack Flight 814.

Outside the crammed airport, it was a warm, chaotic day. A car pulled up in the parking lot. The Pakistan embassy car, whose registration plate read 42 CD 14, had made its way through the busy Kathmandu traffic with three occupants: Mohammad Arshad Cheema, first secretary in the embassy's consulate section, staffer Zia Ansari and a third man. Two of them collected their diplomatic passes which would provide them unrestricted entry into the airport building. Cheema, fifty-two, is an officer familiar to Indian and Nepali authorities in Kathmandu. Officials on both sides say they first came to know of Cheema's role in the Kathmandu embassy after a Sikh militant, arrested from a small hotel in the Nepalese capital with about eighteen kilograms of the explosive RDX in 1998, named Cheema among the people at the Pakistani embassy who he was interacting with. However, Cheema was still not deported from Nepal.

Indian officials say Cheema, who was seen by the airport staff as carrying a small bag, walked through the ground floor lounge with one of his associates, by the X-ray machines, and up the stairs to the departure lounge, where he handed a bag with weapons to Athar. To airport officials, Cheema, who belongs to the Jat community in Pakistan's Punjab province, seems like their usual suspect. But even if there is little concrete evidence that links him with abetment of the hijacking that was to take place soon after, it was clear that on that day, only a very unlucky man would have been caught carrying a bag full of weapons into a plane. There were three policemen and a lady constable at the immigration check point as the passengers lined up. The passengers were in a hurry, but the staff seemed in a greater hurry. One of the men seemed to be flirting with the woman staffer as the crowd hurried through. The metal detector was not working. The baggage was not screened. Most boarding passes were not checked. The passengers were not frisked. Nearly 180 passengers were through, just like that, in minutes.

An hour later, passenger Chander Chhabra ran into a tiny fortune in the departure lounge. The forty-year-old manufacturer of iron pipes from New Delhi was part of a raucous team of sixteen traders who had won a trip to the Himalayan nation in a trade lottery. After enjoying three lovely days of temporary bachelorhood, away from their homes, the young traders were on their way back to New Delhi.

The passengers sat on rows of red, gray and orange chairs in the departure lounge which hummed with laughter and keen conversations. They shuttled between the glittering, glass-panelled snacks counter and their seats and shuffled restlessly in their chairs. Pacing in the lounge, Chhabra bent down to pick up something from the floor. In front of the intricately carved brown wooden doors of the duty free wine shop, he found a thick wad of Indian 500-rupee currency notes.

Either this could be an unexpected bonus — or all these notes could be fake and land the men in big trouble, probably in jail.

Fake Indian currency notes are widely in circulation in Nepal, allegedly printed with the support of Pakistan. The police in India and Nepal are cracking down on people found carrying counterfeit notes, and 500-rupee notes are not welcome in Nepal.

Chhabra and his friends had some idea of the magnitude of the fake money racket in Nepal, and he advised his friends to first count the notes and check each one to see if they were real. The three men huddled in a corner, and started counting the bills, one by one. They did not want to arouse suspicion, so they went into one of the toilets and counted the notes there. Minutes later, they darted out and counted some more bills standing near the snacks counter. They totalled 31,000 rupees.

The men were relieved, all the notes were real. They thought of handing the notes over to the airport authorities, but decided against it: the man who had lost the money seemed to be there, right before them. Prasad Babu was looking frantically all around him, on the seats and on the floor, searching for the wad he had lost minutes ago. Chhabra and two of his friends walked up to him and said: "You seem very anxious. Any problem?"

"I have lost my money. Thirty-one thousand," Babu said, gesturing in the air. The three men handed the notes to him.

Babu did not quite know what to do. He hugged them, started smiling, took out his video camera and took their pictures, and then walked to the duty free shop to buy them an expensive bottle of Scotch. Then they laughed and slapped each other's backs and talked of where they lived in India, where they worked — conversations lost in the crowd of loud voices in the crammed airport lounge. Or, not so lost.

Across the lounge, five men sat expressionless on their cold chairs, barely uttering a word, looking around with a stoic silence. Unknown to Chhabra, one of the five was keeping track of what the Indian group had been doing in the lounge. He had noticed their movements, their baggage, the way they carried themselves. He saw them huddle, he saw them sneak into bathrooms, he saw them whisper in each other's ears. Chhabra and his friends were behaving awkwardly, and the man on the chair was suspicious. This man, one of the four friends of Ibrahim Athar, would tell the Indian men more about those moments eight days later.

He would also tell some passengers that several hundred thousand rupees had been paid to the staff at the Kathmandu airport to organise the hijacking — a claim there is no way to verify.

This six-foot-something muscular hulk, with a wheatish-coloured face and square jaw, was Mohammad Shakir, a man with the kind of athletic V-shaped body that provokes desiring glances from women. He had a scar above the left eyebrow, and terrifying eyes that seemed to pierce right through as he looked at two young boys standing in the lounge. Since the flight was delayed, young Nitin was clutching his boarding card and ferrying the snacks provided by the airline from the snacks counter to his family. As he saw Shakir, he whispered to his cousin Ajay, half in jest, as they stood having a nibble: "Hey, doesn't that man look like a terrorist?" Then they giggled, and hastily turned away their faces as they saw Shakir, out of earshot, staring coldly at them.

A little over an hour later, Nitin would get the terrifying realisation that he was right. And he would realise eight days later that Shakir remembered him, and remembered that moment.

Shakir, believed to be from Sukkur in Pakistan's Sindh province, seemed in his early twenties. He wore a gray T-shirt, dark gray jeans, a blue jersey and Nike sports shoes. There was one white golf bag and at least four dark-coloured backpacks kept near him on the floor. Four other men sat next to him, inconspicuous among the dozens of passengers which included gushing couples returning from honeymoons, grim-faced businessmen and tired looking tourists. Sitting with him was Zahur Ibrahim Mistri of Karachi, lean and around five feet eight inches tall, but less poised than Shakir. Mistri wore a pair of dark gray jeans and light gray jacket, and shuffled in his seat restlessly.

Left-handed Sunny Ahmed Qazi, the fourth in the group, also had an athletic build, an elliptical head, black eyes that seemed to bulge and stare, a broad forehead, thick lips and teeth that appeared discoloured as he spoke. Qazi, who also lives in Karachi, looked around twenty-seven years of age and had unusual marks below both his eyebrows which seemed to be burn marks. They were not. Qazi wore a black T-shirt that had 'Kathmandu' and an intricate design printed on it, apart from black track pants and matching black sports shoes.

The last in the group was Shahid Akhtar Sayeed, also of Karachi, a man with long hair who wore spectacles and had a face with a fair complexion and slight furrows. At about thirty years, he looked slightly older than the others except Athar.

Sayeed had a long sharp nose, drooping shoulders and wore a red T-shirt and trousers with black checks which were soon to be splashed around the front pages of the world's newspapers. Sayeed's face resembled that of Arbaaz Khan, an upcoming Hindi movie actor, brother of Indian superstar Salman Khan. And he loved his smoke.

The five men had travelled on IC 814 at least four times in the preceding months to familiarise themselves with the plane.

As they would later tell their hostages, they had also scoured the Kathmandu and New Delhi airports several times to observe the security arrangements at both airports and the working of the employees. They were all either members of, or linked to, the Harkat-ul Mujahideen, the terrorist group that the burly Maulana belonged to. A plan that had been hatched months ago was set to be executed in a desperate attempt to help Masood Azhar break free of the fifteen-foot walls that had caged him for years in Jammu. As they sat in the airport lounge, they scrutinised the passengers, sized up everyone, and singled out several men who could offer possible resistance to them. According to Indian intelligence, the contents of Cheema's bag had now been shared among the five men.

They sat unnoticed among the boarding card-clutching throngs, with some unusual cabin baggage — apart from new clothes, their bags had ski masks, pistols, knives, hand grenades and a satellite phone.

Far above them, at a height of about 29,000 feet, a wide-bodied Airbus 300 was about to begin a steady descent towards the Tribhuvan International Airport.

Captain Devi Sharan, the commander of the plane, guided the plane as it pierced down the skies at about 145 nautical miles or 270 kilometres per hour. The A300 was a veteran of the skies: it was introduced into the fleet in 1976 and had since made 30,000 landings, notching up 45,000 flying hours. At 15,000 feet, the pilot and co-pilot completed a landing check list. "Descend from 150 to 11,500 and then you are cleared for VOR DME Approach for Runway Two," a clear voice in the Kathmandu ATC tower instructed. The Kathmandu airport, located in a valley and with a landing route flanked on both sides by mountains, is considered a difficult one for landing, though the 10,000-feet runway gives pilots enough room for touchdown. The plane was in what is known as a step descent, in which the plane seems to be going down small steps and then 'walking' for some distance before stepping down again.

The plane touched down at a speed of about 210 kilometres per hour, and soon taxied to a halt. It was 3:45 in the afternoon. Weary passengers who had to sit through hours of delay at New Delhi's international airport slowly walked out and disappeared into the city's tourist-clogged roads. Capt. Sharan and Flight Engineer Anil Jaggia completed the mandatory paperwork, including the filling up of the engine log book and the Pilot Defect Report, and then stepped out to inspect the aircraft.

Capt. Sharan had had a long day on 24 December. He was in Hyderabad with his family — his wife Navneet and daughters Diksha, ten, and Ashna, seven — away from his home in south Delhi where he lived in the Indian Airlines Colony. At five in the morning, he took a flight to New Delhi. In the afternoon, Sharan was in the cockpit again, flying to Kathmandu. The flight was scheduled for 11.15 a.m. but it was delayed by three hours. At the New Delhi airport, his pilot colleague Amartya Basu offered to swap shifts with Sharan and volunteered to fly Flight 814. Sharan declined.

Sharan, thirty-seven, had been flying for twelve years now, and the Airbus 300, which he was flying today, seemed to be his favourite. Apart from a freak incident in the early 1990s when he had to make a belly landing, he had had a smooth career. He was then flying a Boeing 737 as co-pilot on a commercial flight and the crew reportedly forgot to release the wheels before a landing. According to officials, he was taken off flying for a year. Sharan had small town roots. He was born in Karnal in Haryana state. He graduated from the local college and then joined the flying school in the city, often telling his parents he wanted to "fly like a bird."

As he prepared for the return journey from Kathmandu to New Délhi, Sharan had something up his sleeve to make it up to his kids for being late: he was to fly late that night with the family to Sharjah in the United Arab Emirates (U.A.E.) for a Christmas Day vacation and, possibly, a shopping spree. He had hoped to return just in time to Hyderabad to catch the Mumbai-Hyderabad-Sharjah flight.

Sharan did keep to his plans — he reached the U.A.E. that night, only, it was in slightly different circumstances.

And the shopping had to wait. For eight days — from that Friday to the next, he had to muster a lot more than what he had learnt at the Karnal Flying Institute.

As the plane was being cleaned and inspected, Anil Sharma, the day's gentle, ever-smiling senior flight purser, got a fifteen-minute breather from work during the forty-minute halt between the two flights. Sharma had had a less hectic day than the rest of the crew, which came from Hyderabad. He had joined his colleagues in New Delhi.

Standing between the business class galley and the passenger cabin, he took out a plate of a chicken delicacy from one of the racks and dug his teeth into it. It was delicious. Sharma quickly finished it, wiped his mouth and opened the wrapper of another plate.

"Kalpana!" he called out to air hostess Kalpana Majumdar, who stood some distance away. "Why don't you people also have something?"

He took another bite, and tried once again to persuade his colleagues to share his lunch. "Listen, the flight is late. Have a bite now, you never know when you will get to eat."

Sharma would marvel at his words later — like the young boy Nitin in the airport lounge, he had no clue he had just said something prophetic.

The announcer's voice echoed across the departure lounge. Finally, Flight 814 was ready to leave. Ibrahim Athar and his four colleagues got up and got ready. The passengers were rushing to the large glass-panelled brown gate where a lone policeman was trying to organise them into a single file before they walked the long gallery towards the plane.

The crowd was restive. Most people were unhappy forming a line and waiting, again, after endless hours of waiting. Many shopping-weary people had a lot of cabin baggage and they were not sure they would get enough space in the luggage compartments to keep their bags — so they wanted to rush to their seats and occupy space first. Several people snapped at others who were jostling.

Suddenly, a man's voice rang across the crowd's clamour.

"Let them go! Let them go quickly!" he hollered to the guard as he gestured with his hands to open the doors.

Daman Soni turned and looked at the man with gratitude. Those who noticed him closely enough would remember exactly what he looked like: around forty-five years of age, he wore a gray suit and a white shirt. He was dark and stocky. Officials at the Tribhuvan International Airport wear gray suits as part of their uniform but no one knew who the man was, or whether his action was linked to the imminent hijacking in any way.

He shouted again.

"Open the door! Let the passengers go!" he shouted with authority. The guard opened the door and the passengers rushed out into the long gallery leading to the plane. The plane was about two hundred feet away and the rush began again as the impatient travellers stood uncomfortably beside the plane at the foot of the step ladder, waiting for their turn to board. The staffer there asked everyone to form a queue.

A few passengers say the man in the gray suit appeared again, and shouted: "Please start boarding, it's all right!"

The crowd marched in. Air hostesses welcomed them inside the aircraft. The passengers settled down. Several started clicking pictures, others took out their HandyCams and zoomed in on friends and family. The cabin crew started explaining safety procedures. Capt. Sharan was ready for take-off. Seated comfortably, passengers stopped grumbling about the seemingly never-ending delays in Indian flights.

Soon they would also have the right to grumble about something no booking clerk would tell them: targeted twelve times, Indian Airlines was apparently already the most hijacked airline in the world.

That number would become thirteen in less than an hour.

THE PREPARATION

*The hijacking plot is hatched in Karachi, fake passports
are made in Mumbai and a bank is robbed there,
and the players collect in Kathmandu*

Abdul Latif Adam Momin would have done well to step
into the restaurant business run by some of his more
affluent relatives. He could have been a shareholder in his
half-brother's hugely popular joint opposite the office of the
Mumbai police commissioner. But Latif, or Patel, as he was
popularly known, turned out to be the prodigal son in his
family — chased and hunted down, ironically, by the same
police commissioner's men.

When terror guru Masood Azhar's brother Ibrahim
Athar made the long distance call to Mumbai on the afternoon of 24 December, minutes after he checked in for the
Indian Airlines flight in Kathmandu, the lanky Latif was
the man at the other end, speaking on a cellular phone. Latif
was in charge of a small but important operation of the
Harkat-ul Mujahideen in Mumbai. With limited men and
resources, and a small room in Mumbai's predominantly

[1]

Muslim neighbourhood of Jogeshwari, he was assigned the task of planning ways to secure Azhar's release. He was not the first to be given the task. Several attempts had been made to free Azhar since his 1994 arrest. Some of these attempts provoked international attention because they included the abductions of foreign citizens: in June 1994, October 1994 and July 1995. The last attempt was the one that grabbed the most international attention: a group calling itself Al Faran, believed to be an affiliate of Maulana Azhar's group, was blamed for the 1995 kidnapping of six Western tourists who were trekking in Kashmir's Pahalgam district. The kidnappers demanded the release of Azhar and twenty other jailed comrades. India refused. Two of the tourists were killed, one escaped and the other three are still missing, presumed dead.

All efforts to free Azhar had failed, and Latif, an Indian national, was asked by his bosses in Karachi, Pakistan, to plan an airplane hijack from Mumbai's Sahar International Airport. Latif found that impossible, so Kathmandu was chosen.

Nepal seemed an easy target for a hijacker. The country of simple people and low crime levels does not have a professional intelligence and security set-up. Many officers have been trained in India, but since 1994, a powerful lobby in the country's police force started opposing the over-bearing influence of Indian police agencies on Nepal's police. Among the alternatives the Nepali authorities sought out was Britain's security service MI-5, an association that diluted the cooperation between security officials in India and Nepal. Pakistani officials also tried to persuade the Nepalese government to accept police training from Islamabad, but it is not known how far the cooperation materialised.

[2]

However, over the last ten years, Nepal became extremely vulnerable to Islamic guerillas, a threat that Nepalese officials say they are now looking at with seriousness. According to unofficial estimates, a significant part of the local tourist infrastructure, including hotels, guest houses, restaurants and travel agencies are owned by or affiliated to Dawood Ibrahim, the mob boss who operates from Karachi and Dubai. The lack of a visa regime between India and Pakistan makes it very easy for Islamic militants trained in Pakistan to fly to Nepal and then cross into India by road.

While Latif's men were working on the hijacking, the police commissioner's men were working hard as well. The police had been tipped off about the existence of Harkat-ul Mujahideen members in Mumbai and were trying to track them down.

The trail to Latif came from an unexpected source: Mumbai's birds. Days before the 24 December afternoon, Indian security agencies were listening in on calls made from a cellular telephone in Mumbai using a pre-paid SIM card, which allows the user to make calls that are not listed on bills. From his conversations, the man seemed shady and investigators believed he could be linked to the new setup of the Harkat-ul Mujahideen in Mumbai the police were after. On 22 December, investigators' wires picked him up again, and attempts started once more to pin down his exact location. This time the sleuths had run into luck: the suspect was talking to an associate, and there were dozens of raucous birds in the background. There were only two places in the city where such loud bird voices could be heard — the Kamala Nehru Park and the expansive R.A. Milk Colony. These were huge areas to scour, but still great leads. The stakeout began. Another investigators' team confirmed that the same cell phone had been used to frequently call numbers in Karachi. Days later, he was spotted at the R.A. Milk Colony and his surveillence eventually led investigators to Latif.

A tape of fiery speeches of Masood Azhar had attracted Latif to the Harkat-ul Mujahideen in Jeddah, Saudi Arabia, where he had gone to work after living in poverty for years. In 1995, he was sent for weapons training to a camp at the Khaled bin Waled training centre in Afghanistan. His 124 colleagues at the 40-day course included Pakistanis, Indians, British, and one American convert to Islam. In 1996, he was driven blindfolded in a pickup van for three hours from Islamabad to a camp belonging to the Inter Services Intelligence. Years later, he became the key contact for the hijackers in Mumbai.

The hijacking is believed to have been planned in Karachi by Abdul Rauf, younger brother of Maulana Masood and Ibrahim Athar, and Yusuf Azhar, the Maulana's brother-in-law, also believed to be in Karachi. Their initial plans to free Masood in a jailbreak by digging a tunnel had failed miserably, and work on the hijacking began in June 1999. It was a tedious job. Nepalese national Gopal Bhimbahadur Maan, called Yusuf Nepali in his circles, was roped in to do the local footwork. Nepali was a key man — he had the right contacts, he could pull the right strings; in his own little area, he was king. Nepali was to be the sixth hijacker. Shahid Akhtar Sayeed, one of the four men at the airport with Masood's brother, met Nepali and his associate Sajid Tibeti in June 1999 and asked them to scout for safe hiding grounds. They did. There was a flurry of travel: Latif went by train to Calcutta and then crossed the Bangladeshi border illegally to reach Dhaka in July 1999, Abdul Rauf went to Kathmandu, and from there reached the Bangladeshi capital. A grand meeting had been planned in a madrassa. Everyone was there — Maulana Masood's two brothers, key troubleshooter Abdul Latif, and the four men who would help Ibrahim Athar carry out the plan: Shahid Akhtar Sayeed, Sunny Ahmed Qazi, Zahur Ibrahim Mistri and Mohammad Shakir. Abdul Rauf did most of the talking. The final details of the hijacking plan were worked out, duties were assigned, and the dangers were assessed.

The meeting over, Latif and Qazi returned to India through the land border, travelling through the towns of Siliguri, Darjeeling, Jalpaiguri and Patna before they took a crowded long distance train to Mumbai. Qazi waited in the city as Latif got to work on the tasks assigned to him. By 18 August he got four fake passports and driving licenses made for Maulana Masood's brother Ibrahim Athar and his four associates. It wasn't a difficult task — Latif went to Suresh Bhatnathe of the Seven Travel Services in central Mumbai, part of a well-oiled network that he and several others had been using in Mumbai's unnoticed bylanes to get hundreds of people fake passports, ration cards and new identities to make them new persons — all for a fee. It also seemed ridiculously simple: when people came applying for new passports, the agents took their original documents, affixed pictures of false applicants, and sent the forms to the Regional Passport Office. According to government regulations, passport officials wait for forty days to let police officials verify the aplication details. The passport agents bribed clerks at the passport office to quickly process the forms, then bribed policemen to give favourable reports or delay their reports and let the 40-day deadline get over — or bribed postmen who were asked to see that the reports never reached the passport office.

The scam worked at such fine levels that it was difficult to detect it — two fake passports were made out for Ibrahim Athar from the Mumbai passport office under two names within two days. One of them was issued in the name of Ahmed Ali Mohammad Ali Shaikh, the other for Jawed Amjad Siddiqi, on 18 and 20 August. The pictures on both forms were identical. The application for Shaikh listed his date of birth as 10 October 1967, and the document for Siddiqi had 19 February 1969 as the birthdate. The cities of birth were shown as Muradabad and Mumbai. Both of Athar's passports were signed by the same officer — J.D. Poojary, a superintendent in the regional passport office. Fake passports were similarly made for the others for all their travel until the plan was executed.

What Ibrahim Athar and the rest of his accomplices did after the Dhaka meeting is not known, but most of the gang reunited in Mumbai in October 1999.

Something else happened in the meanwhile. On the morning of 6 October, four men pushed their way into a car in the Malad neighbourhood and forced the driver to go to Borivili. They stopped outside the Maharashtra State Cooperative Bank and stormed in, and as horrified customers watched, the men escaped with about Rs. 750,000 in currency notes. As he rushed out, one of the armed men also snatched the identity card of a bank employee. Latif would later tell his interrogators that the money was used to sustain the Harkat-ul Mujahideen men in the city, though the amount seemed tiny compared with the level of their planned operations. The identity card would be used later to buy a pre-paid SIM card for Latif's cellular phone which would become a three-way lifeline of information between Abdul Rauf in Karachi, Latif in Mumbai and the five men in the Indian Airlines plane.

[6]

From Mumbai, the hectic trips continued. On 1 November 1999, Latif and Shahid Akhtar Sayeed flew from Mumbai to Calcutta, then took a train to New Jalpaiguri and travelled by road to Kathmandu. There Latif contacted his associates Sajid Tibeti and Yusuf Nepali, and returned to Mumbai leaving behind Sayeed. A month later, on 1 December, Latif escorted Ibrahim Athar and Mohammad Shakir, the muscled henchman, to Kathmandu after travelling by train to Gorakhpur town in Uttar Pradesh near the Indian border with Nepal, and boarding a bus from there for Kathmandu. A week later, Sunny Ahmad Qazi and Zahur Ibrahim Mistri followed the same route, taking the road route to Kathmandu via Gorakhpur on 8 December. Now all the five men who were to board the plane were in Kathmandu, staying in different places and changing hotels frequently.

On 13 December, Yusuf Nepali went to the travel agency Everest Travels and Tours, just down the road from the opulent palace of King Birendra, and bought three economy class tickets for the 27 December Indian Airlines flight to New Delhi from Kathmandu. Two other business class tickets were bought from the Gorkha Travel Agency. But there was a sudden change of plan on 13 December: all the tickets were changed to 24 December. Later on 13 December, Ibrahim Athar called a meeting in the Kathmandu zoo. The final plan was decided. The conspirators huddled together in a desolate place inside the zoo. The names of the five passengers were written on five separate pieces of paper and Ibrahim Athar picked one to decide who would take the maximum risk of taking arms inside the plane. He picked himself.

All plans in place, Latif left for New Delhi on 17 December, travelling on Indian Airlines under the assumed name

[7]

of A.L.A. Momin, and returned to Mumbai by train. He kept calling Ibrahim Athar and his men on his cell phone several times a day. In Kathmandu, the men kept changing hotels.

Some time before noon on 24 December, Ibrahim Athar drove to the Tribhūvan International Airport alone, and checked in. Then, before he climbed the stairs to the immigration check counter, he walked to the phones. He called Latif, and then his four associates who were in a hotel in the city. He was ready, he said.

DAY

1

==

*With so-called decision-makers in Delhi paralysed,
a passenger is killed ... and the plane nearly crashes
twice, with the captain begging to be allowed to land
in Lahore and the U.A.E.*

The engines roared to life, the panels inside the Airbus
300 cockpit lit up and Captain Devi Sharan settled into his
seat adjusting his headphones. The beacons outside the
aircraft came to life. Flight IC 814 was readying for take-off,
back to New Delhi, after a 40-minute stopover at
Kathmandu. Capt. Sharan, the young commander of the
plane, was on the left, co-pilot Captain Rajinder Kumar
Goud to his right, and Flight Engineer Anil K. Jaggia was
in the centre on his seat behind them. Both pilots looked
hard at their Jeppesen Approach Plates — complicated
maps with lots of circles and lines which show flight routes
to pilots. They quickly completed a technical check list that
is mandatory for pilots before ascent and descent of an

aircraft, and Jaggia checked the cabin pressure from a panel to his right, moving his chair on little rails. Everything in place, Capt. Sharan ordered the cabin crew to secure all doors. The plane began to taxi down the runway before its take-off. In the passenger cabin, several people had just finished clicking each other's pictures as they posed in their seats. The flying time to New Delhi was an hour and twenty-five minutes, and, despite a frustrating three-hour delay, the 178 passengers would be just in time for noisy Christmas Eve parties. Several corporate executives would be sucked into work right away, going to their offices to check if their busy control rooms set up for the Y2K computer bug were in shape. Many had to plan their New Year's vacations. Most others just wanted to snuggle in cosy beds after the tiring day. Apart from 154 Indians and eight Nepalese, there were many foreign tourists as well — one Canadian, one American, four Swiss, four Spanish, one Belgian, one Japanese, one Austrian, two French and one Italian.

The plane took off into the mountain-peppered horizon. It was about quarter-past four in the evening. Anil Sharma, the senior flight purser, was serving in the business class cabin, slightly overworked because he had two people less on duty that day. The air hostesses — Kobita Mukherjee, Kalpana Majumdar, Rajni Shekhar, Sapnarani Menon and Tapa Debnath — walked up and down the economy class aisle pushing trolleys as they served drinks to the passengers. Over the next forty minutes, most passengers were served their food trays, with a rice preparation for the vegetarian and chicken for the non-vegetarian. Inside the cockpit, the pilots and the flight engineer put the plane on autopilot, letting the aircraft charge through the skies on its own, and sat back. Cruising at about seven nautical miles (thirteen kilometres) per minute, the Airbus had flown over Bharatpur town in Nepal, then entered Indian territory over the border town of Bhairahawa, and taken about ten minutes to reach a point about eighty-five nautical miles (158 kilometres) from Lucknow.

Tea was on its way. Apart from the pilots, one passenger in the front row of the business class was also waiting for the cockpit crew to be served. Ibrahim Athar was ready for the strike. He had only one moment before the pilot would again secure the cockpit door mechanically, from inside. Anil Sharma gently pushed open the cockpit door with tea cups. He handed them one by one to Capt. Sharan, Capt. Rajinder and Jaggia. Then he took a few steps and opened the door to step out again. In the split second that he turned with his back towards the passengers, Athar sprang from his seat. Passenger Ramesh Grover, sitting right in the front in seat 1B, saw the masked man behind Sharma, a familiar face for him from several previous flights on the Kathmandu route. He thought it was a prankster. With the hint of a knowing smile on his face, Grover gestured to Sharma with his eyebrows, as if saying: There is someone behind you. Sharma swiftly turned around to see a portly man with a slight hunch, wearing a suit and a red ski mask pointing a revolver at him, almost from point-blank range. He had a grenade in the other hand, the pin taken off and dangling between his fingers.

"*Hilna nahin* (Don't move). We're taking over the aircraft," Athar said brusquely, and added: "*Hamari aapse koi dushmani nahin hai*" (We have no enmity against you). He then pushed the half-open cockpit door and entered. As they heard the thud of the closing door, the three men inside the cockpit turned their heads and saw an unexpected sight: a masked, edgy man with a revolver in his left hand and a grenade in his right hand. For a moment, Capt. Sharan thought it was some kind of a year-end prank, and the man was a crank or a joker. Then they saw the gun. It seemed real. "*Koi hoshiyari nahin karega, varna hum tayyare ko uda denge*" (No one try to act smart, otherwise we will blow up the plane), he shouted above the plane's loud drone in a nervous, gruff voice. "This is a grenade and this is a revolver in my hands. The aircraft is under our control. Fly west."

Many things happened in that short, frenzied moment. Another man — Sunny Ahmed Qazi — got up from his seat in the business class, stepped into the toilet, and when he stepped out he was wearing a black monkey cap that left only his eyes and nose visible.

"Hijack!" he shouted. The stunned passengers did not know how to react. The next instruction followed immediately. "Heads down!" In the economy class, the three other men got up together, almost like clockwork, flailing their weapons in the air and shouting in a disjointed chorus. Sunny Ahmed Qazi took a few quick steps to come to the kitchen area between the business and economy classes, and pushed aside a startled air hostess. Then he raised his arms, displaying a gun in one hand and a grenade in the other. It took a while to register — after all, the passengers were being hijacked for the first time in their lives. Rajeev Ahuja, thirty-four, a tall, nervous businessman from New Delhi, frantically asked air hostess Sapnarani Menon, who stood near Qazi: "What is going on?" She stepped closer and said in a hushed voice: "It's a hijack." Most people were having their food and several could barely hear a word in the din, just see men with masks and arms. It could well be a Christmas surprise from Indian Airlines, some thought, and kept munching as they watched what they

[12]

thought was a colourful charade. Others thought it was a practical joke by students who were returning from Nepal with toy guns, and started laughing.

These were no students. These were no toy guns. Within minutes, Ibrahim Athar and his four masked associates transformed into the mysterious, unknown, faceless names they would remain for long, tortuous days: Athar himself was now 'Chief,' Sunny Ahmed Qazi was 'Burger,' Mohammad Shakir was 'Shankar,' Shahid Akhtar Sayeed was 'Doctor,' and Zahur Ibrahim Mistri was 'Bhola.' For the five men, there wasn't a moment to waste. A meticulous drill rehearsed several times over had to be completed. Bhola, holding a knife, walked to the public address system in the middle galley and tried to press the button to make an announcement. It wouldn't work. Purser Anil Sharma, now walking precariously from the business class towards the economy class, was summoned again to help. Sharma pressed the button again, but it did not work. Bhola got very angry.

"*Kuchch karo, kuchch bhi karo*. (Do something. Anything) I need to make an announcement," he said.

Next to him, Shankar pointed a pistol at Sharma.

"What happened to this thing?"

"It is jammed," Sharma said, struggling with the mike.

"Why?"

"I don't know. I haven't done it deliberately."

He growled again, asking for the hand-held mike. Sharma walked to a nearby row and opened the luggage compartment to pull out a red microphone kept for emergencies. A revolver still in his hand, Shankar held the mike with three fingers and brought it to his mouth.

"This plane has been hijacked. Heads down! Roll up the tables! Put down the food trays!" Shankar screamed, his

[13]

well-built, muscular body towering above the passengers. The other hijackers barked similar instructions as they took up positions some distance away from each other, three holding knives. They started pushing the food trolleys down the aisle, wheeling them to the galleries and toppling over at least two. They yelled at passengers left and right, asking them to tuck their heads between their legs. Bhola, Shankar and Doctor walked down the aisle, bellowing commands, angrily throwing the food trays below the seats and slamming up the foldable tables. Several men were slapped or kicked in the shoulders for responding slowly to the commands. Some people were thrashed for the wrong reason — Tamil passenger Prasad Babu and his six colleagues from Vellore town did not understand a word of Hindi and thus did not know what the hijackers' commands were. They were flummoxed as they were slapped and kicked.

Many women were weeping, and all of them were asked to cover their heads with saris and dupattas. For the passengers, no doubt remained now: their lives were in danger. There was silence in the aircraft, even the puzzled children were surprisingly quiet. Row upon row of heads went down as if a wave had swept through the plane flattening them. Those who could not bow low, just kept their heads on the foldable plastic food tables. Those who were obese or stiff and could not do even that, just bent their heads. Submission was complete; within a minute, the hijackers had taken over the aircraft. The four hijackers walked threateningly down the aisle, often running, their shoes thumping across the aircraft floor.

Among the passengers was Gajendra Man Tamarkar, a pashmina shawl seller from Kathmandu. Carrying a consignment of pashmina shawls, he had reached the airport too late to catch a Royal Nepal Airways flight to New Delhi. The airline officials suggested he fly Indian Airlines instead, and tempted Tamarkar, who weighs about 150 kilograms, by saying that the food there was great. Tamarkar would be in the news a lot over the next several days — but for all the wrong reasons. And the food wouldn't exactly be great.

In the cockpit, Chief hollered his first instructions: "Take us to Lahore." Capt. Sharan replied: "There might not be enough fuel," but obeyed and cruised in the direction of the Pakistani town that has been a favourite destination of many hijackers of Indian Airlines planes in the past. Then he requested Chief to allow him to inform the passengers and the ground control, to which the hijackers' leader nodded in approval. About seven minutes after Athar had walked into the cockpit brandishing his weapons, Capt. Sharan informed the flight control in Varanasi of the hijacking on the radio transmitter on an open frequency that can be heard by all.

Then Capt. Sharan went on the public address system to announce a terse message: "The plane is being hijacked. Please cooperate."

Hundreds of kilometres away at the Air Traffic Control Tower in New Delhi's Indira Gandhi International Airport, the radio crackled. A voice from the Varanasi airport snapped: "IC 814 has been hijacked." The ATC had had a busier day than usual. Hours earlier, the radar had detected aircraft Jupiter 123 making an unauthorised entry into Indian airspace. The aircraft was warned and the security drill was quickly put in place, but by the time the plane was forcelanded, it turned out the unauthorised entry was a mock exercise. It took the ATC some seconds to realise that the hijack was not a drill. The secondary radar systems

[15]

started beeping and the hijacked plane appeared in the form of a red flower on the console. To confirm that the hijack had taken place, the pilot conveyed the emergency code 7500 on the ATC transponder.

Then, Capt. Sharan's hoarse voice was heard for the first time after the distress call: "They have bombs, dynamite, AK47. *Boss keh rahe hain unki manzil aage hai* (Boss is saying their destination is further ahead). They want us to go to Lahore."

At 28,000 feet, two thousand feet above the hijacked plane and about forty nautical miles (seventy-four kilometres) ahead, there was another aircraft flying in the direction of New Delhi which should have heard the distress call along with the other planes in the vicinity. Sitting inside this special Indian Air Force plane, protected by commandos, was another protagonist of the story, the man whose hand would be forced by the five hijackers eight days later: India's Prime Minister Atal Behari Vajpayee. Returning from a political rally in Bihar, he was accompanied by Civil Aviation Minister Sharad Yadav, another key figure in the hijacking saga. Unknown both to the hijackers and the prime minister, Vajpayee and the five men were starting together in mid-air a gruelling rollercoaster drama of violence, revenge and emotional outpourings that they would end thousands of kilometres away from each other. Vajpayee was embarking on one of the toughest crises of his life.

Despite being so close to the hijacked aircraft himself, he was not informed of the crisis and is believed to have learnt about the hijacking after word spread across the country. The prime minister's air force plane is equipped with state-of-the-art communication equipment — apart from contact through a radio transmitter and a satellite phone, the occupant of the plane can be contacted from a fixed telephone line as well. But Capt. Sharan's messages about the hijacking, the demand to fly to Lahore, and the shortage of fuel, were apparently not conveyed to the prime minister. Capt. R.N. Singh, Indian Airlines general manager for the northern region who was commanding a flight in the neighbourhood, was among the pilots who heard the distress call and spoke to Capt. Sharan to calm him down.

In the hijacked plane, a horrific calm had hushed the aircraft. The terrified, often trembling passengers had their heads between their legs. Some started throwing up, either due to the pressure on their stomachs so soon after having eaten or in plain anxiety. Several women cried uncontrollably. Watching them, some anxious men started crying as well, their wet cheeks merging with the columns of feet and heads below the seats. The children obeyed silently, anxiously watching their parents bow meekly before five rude strangers. The four men in the economy classes snatched the cameras from all passengers, even searching hand baggages for any cameras there, and exposed all film rolls. When a passenger was slow to obey, Bhola shouted: "*Shaadi mein aae ho kya?*" (Have you come to a wedding?)

All male passengers were frisked. The bags were searched. Forks and knives — anything that could be used as a weapon — were removed from the plates. Baggage was thrown into the business class. Then, Burger shouted to the air hostesses in the front: "*Inke muh par kapda bandho!*" (Tie cloth on their faces). There was no cloth other than the white napkins laid on the head-rests on the seats. When the stewards said a napkin each would not be enough, Burger asked them to tie two napkins together and then wrap them like blindfolds. The air hostesses started the tedious process of covering the eyes of the male passengers one by one — in normal times they would have looked funny with the napkins forming funny hoods over their faces.

Burger walked up the aisle and stepped inside the cockpit. He greeted Chief with a military-style salute, took a quick look around and said: "Sir, *peechche sab control ho gaya hai.*" (Everything is under control at the back).

Chief turned to the commander and made his orders clear: "*Lahore chaliye. Varna hum tayyare ko uda denge*" (Go to Lahore. Otherwise we will blow up the plane).

Minutes later, Step Two of the hijack began. The hijackers started hollering down the aisles, asking all passengers to get up from their seats. The business class passengers were herded from their spacious seats to the economy class, and the economy class passengers were asked to shift to the rear seats. The stewards sat in the front rows of the economy class. There was some chaos in the aircraft as dozens of terrified people got up from their seats and walked briskly past the hijackers, not having the courage to look at their masked faces, and walked towards the rear looking for seats they thought were safe.

Honeymooners Vishal and Kavita Sharma, who had got married less than two weeks ago on 13 December, briskly walked on but stopped when they saw several seats vacant in the middle rows. Kavita whispered: "Let's sit down here, who knows they might blow up the back portion or something." Gradually, the passengers settled down and fastened their seat belts, coming to terms with their mid-air captivity. One young woman started throwing up, and an air hostess rushed as Doctor ordered water. But as the woman wiped her face and brought the bottle near her lips,

Shankar shouted sternly from the back: *"Zyada paani mat do! Abhi do-teen din tak zaroorat paregi!* (Don't give too much water! We are going to need this for two or three days!") Then he turned and started his patrol again, one finger slid inside the grenade pin to let it dangle precariously. The business class was now vacant; this would now become the hijackers' home. They reserved the two toilets in the front for their use. Then they took their bags to the business class, and ordered the stewards to carry the passengers' luggage there as well. For a long time, the air hostesses continued opening luggage compartments one after the other, lugging heavy bags and suitcases up the aisle to the business class.

One of the passengers, Dr. Anita Joshi, was having a severe pain in the stomach and asked Doctor if she could go to the toilet. He refused and went away. A minute later, he appeared again with a Paracetamol tablet and offered it to her.

"What is this? Paracetamol does not work for stomach aches," she said. Doctor said : "How do you know all this?"

"I am a doctor," Dr. Joshi told the hijacker called Doctor. She would have a lot to do with the five men.

There was feverish activity, and a lot of chaos, in New Delhi. The ATC quickly put the hijack drill in action: the Works Supervisory Officer was informed and he conveyed word to the Aerodrome Committee, the lowest in the hier-archical rungs of government panels that work in an avia-tion emergency. Airport officials then hunted frantically for the telephone numbers of top officials — some had been changed — and when they were contacted, the officials knew little of what was to be done next. Some reportedly asked the airport staff if they needed to come to the airport at all. The next step would be for the Crisis Management Group (CMG), a core team of decision-makers headed by the cabinet secretary, to meet within thirty minutes of information of the hijacking coming in.

Meanwhile, with a gun to his head, Capt. Sharan kept communicating with two officials at the control tower in New Delhi, which takes over flight control from Varanasi after an aircraft crosses Lucknow. At ATC, two officials were talking to Sharan. "They want to go to Lahore, they want to go to Lahore" Capt. Sharan told the two ATC officials several times. It was nearly 5:20 in the evening. With the plane now near New Delhi, the level-headed pilot had a small plan of his own up his sleeve. Desperately trying to buy time, Capt. Sharan slowed down the aircraft's speed, from the normal Airbus speed of about 460 nautical miles (850 kilometres) per hour, to about 360 nautical miles (666 kilometres) per hour. Capt. Sharan seemed to be delaying reaching a place called Point Ansari on his map, equidistant from both Lahore and Amritsar, from where he would have to turn left for Lahore, rather than right and straight for Amritsar. If he was able to avoid flying towards Lahore, he wanted to take the plane to the Raja Sansi Airport in Amritsar, where officials have successfully handled several hijackings in the past. If it reached Amritsar, the hijacked plane would have travelled 596 nautical miles (1,102 kilometres) from the point where the five men took over.

Thousands of feet below Capt. Sharan's aircraft, government officials were offering a brilliant example of how not to tackle a hijacking crisis in which nearly two hundred lives were endangered. Prime Minister Vajpayee's jet touched down at the Palam Technical Airport at about 5:20 p.m. As a tired Vajpayee stepped out shielded by commandos of the Special Protection Group (SPG) and sirens echoed across the airport, one of his waiting aides rushed to him with a small slip of paper that would give him the first information on the hostage-taking. Vajpayee's aides said that he did not know of the hijacking while he was on the plane — even though Capt. Sharan was speaking on an open frequency. In an era of sophisticated mobile and satellite phones, the prime minister of the world's largest democracy had to be handed a slip of paper forty minutes after the event to be informed of one of the most gripping crises he faced since coming to power. Even the top officials on the ground, or the prime minister's staff, did not find the hijacking an important enough event to pick up the phone and call the leader.

In the cockpit of IC 814, the pilot made another feeble attempt, and asked Chief whether he could land the plane in New Delhi for refuelling.

"*Dilli ki baat mat karo* (Don't even mention Delhi)," Chief retorted. Capt. Sharan contacted New Delhi again, and requested the tower to get air clearance from Lahore. New Delhi responded soon, saying the Lahore runway was closed and the authorities there were not giving permission to IC 814 to land. Capt. Sharan told Chief there was no option but to land in Amritsar. But Chief was adamant.

In New Delhi, unaware of the mid-air drama, journalists were working on endless stories on the Y2K bug and the millennium, weaving dark theories about the possible catastrophe that the computer error was about to bring. Then the news agency teleprinters flashed their first few lines on the hijacking. Information was scarce, and few officials were available. Dozens of callers jammed the lines of the Indian Airlines spokesman's office. For the lucky few, there would be a voice at the other end that would give the little details that were available. Cars dashed out of television networks' offices, reporters rushed out. This could be a real big story. Y2K would wait. At the news desks, journalists continued a difficult guessing game of where the plane would head next.

In another part of the city, a convoy of white Ambassador cars was speeding on roads cleared by over-zealous policemen. The prime minister reached his residence at 7, Race Course Road at 5.35 p.m. and asked senior Cabinet colleagues to see him for an urgent meeting. A few kilometres away in Rajiv Gandhi Bhavan, where the civil aviation ministry is located, the top officials who form the CMG — including Cabinet Secretary Prabhat Kumar, Civil Aviation Secretary Ravinder Gupta, intelligence officials and the director of the National Security Guards (NSG) Nikhil Kumar — were yet to arrive. The staff readied a conference room, the canteen was alerted. This was going to be the first of several long nights. A few minutes after 5:30, the CMG started its meeting. The plane seemed headed for Amritsar, but there was little the group seemed to be able to do. Negotiators were not ready. Commandos were not given the orders. The crisis group was itself not ready for a crisis. According to some accounts, the officials asked the staff to pull out old dusty files on previous hijackings at Amritsar to understand what officials did then, and figure out what to do now.

In the plane, Capt. Sharan contacted the ATC at Amritsar at 6:18 p.m. He said desperately: "CFM (Confirm) with OPLA (Lahore). We are in contact with OPLA. OPLA is not allowing us to land and we have only forty minutes' fuel. They are insisting (on) us to go to OPLA and they are not allowing us to land on Indian soil." Three minutes later, he was back on the radio: "Intentions are very strong as they have to land in OPLA only. Otherwise, they are ready to crash anywhere. They do not want to land in India."

At the Rajiv Gandhi Bhavan in New Delhi, cigarette smoke wafted inside a room where the CMG sat studying the crisis — unfortunately doing little else. There was no quick, coherent, crack decision by some of the leading minds of India's bureaucracy. The kitchen staff worked like clockwork supplying black coffee and snacks to the bureaucrats — by the end of the crisis, they would have consumed more than three hundred cups to keep awake through tension-filled nights. Hordes of journalists waited outside in a gallery. From time to time, they pounced expectantly on any tired-looking official emerging out of the room with dishevelled hair and tie askew.

An official at the CMG gave the clearance to a crack team of fifty commandos of the NSG, comparable to the best anti-hijack teams in the world. They were to leave for Amritsar in their IL76 plane but the heavy anti-hijacking equipment would take time to load, and officials at NSG wished the clearance had come earlier from the dilly-dallying bureaucrats.

Capt. Sharan blurted out more desperate messages as he approached closer to the India-Pakistan border. At 6:26 p.m., he said: "We have fuel only for half-an-hour. Please coordinate with OPLA. Please get our permission to land at OPLA. They (hijackers) are very silly and they will kill us one by one." Five minutes later, he said: "Their conscience is bad, they have already selected ten people to kill." Capt. Sharan was mostly repeating what Chief asked him to say.

Authorities at Amritsar sealed the Raja Sansi Airport, barring even journalists from entering. The police started trooping in. But authorities there still had no instructions from New Delhi on how officials should deal with the crisis. In the state capital of Chandigarh, Director-General of Police Sarbjeet Singh had heard of the hijacking about twenty minutes ago — not from the CMG but from television. In Amritsar, District Commissioner Narinder Singh went into an emergency session with Inspector-General of Police J.P. Birdi, Senior Superintendent of Police Parampal Singh Sidhu and Airport Director Vijay Mulakar. This would be the last big assignment for Birdi in the Amritsar range — he had received orders for his transfer a few days ago.

As minutes ticked by, Capt. Sharan made the last request at 6:32 p.m. to the ATC for a landing at Lahore: "There is only fifteen minutes of fuel left. Make sure we land in OPLA as they want to land in OPLA and otherwise not anywhere in India."

But Lahore was firm on denying permission. IC 814 was now over Point Ansari, the crucial aerial milestone from where he would head to either Lahore or Amritsar. Capt. Sharan persuaded the hijackers that he would land in Amritsar, quickly refuel and fly off. Chief had little option, and he reluctantly agreed. The plane turned towards Amritsar. At about 6:35 p.m., Capt. Sharan began his descent towards the 9,150 feet runway, a gun still by his shoulder. Nine minutes later, he touched down. Even as the plane slowed down and taxied on the runway, the pilot was on the radio with the ground control, often rambling on and speaking incoherent sentences in his anxiety: "They want fuel tanker. If they are going to park on runway itself, if you have to position us, fuel tanker, fuel tanker. They have everything. Revolvers, AK-47, grenades ... everything in hand, everything open. They want refuelling is (sic) immediately done."

[24]

But Chief was edgy. This could be a trap. He knew exactly what the Indian authorities would do in such a situation — a planeload of commandos would land and in a swift operation of only a few minutes, would try to storm the plane. He was immensely helped by the tardiness of Indian officials, because no such action happened. But he asked Capt. Sharan not to shut off the engine or to stop at one point. To keep another plane from landing, Chief asked Capt. Sharan to taxi on the runway, back and forth. He would do this for nearly an hour, as Chief poked his gun alternately into the backs of the three crew members.

Sitting in Karachi, Abdul Rauf was getting tense. There had been no word on whether the aircraft had landed at Amritsar. According to the plan, his elder brother and the other four men were supposed to call Abdul Latif, their man in Bombay. Suddenly, his phone rang. It was Latif all right.

Latif: *Kya haal hai?* (How are you?)

Rauf: *Allah ka shukar hai, koi nayee taza koi khabar hai?* (It's Allah's grace. Any fresh news?)

Latif: *Haan hai, aapke paas koi khabar aai hai?* (Yes. Do you have any news?)

Rauf: *Nahin, mere paas to nahin hai. Bhai ne raafta nahin kiya?* (No I don't. Has Brother contacted you yet?)

Latif: *Nahin ... Khabrein to hain kafi kuchch lekin vo yeh hai ki saat baje utra tha jahan maine bataya.* (No ... There is a lot of news but the main thing is that it landed at seven o'clock at the place I told you.)

Rauf: *Achcha.* (Yes ...)

Latif: *Aur ye unse baatchit kar rahe hain. Ain apne unko kareeb aane nahin de rahe hain. Keh rahe hain door se hi baat karo.* (And these people are talking to them. [Athar and his men] are not letting them come close. They are asking them to talk from a distance.)

Rauf: *Haan. Doosra, agar bhai ka ab tak raafta hota hai, abhi thodi ... to bhai se kaho fauran chhor deve ilake, kyonki yahan par jo khabrein aa rahi hain uske mutabik yeh hai ki ye tayyari kar rahe hain.* (Yes. Second thing, if you are able to contact Brother ... tell Brother to immediately leave the area, because the information I have here is that they are making preparations [for a commando raid].)

Latif: *Achcha.* (OK.)

Rauf: *Andar* (inaudible) *ho rahi hai. Aur jo issee line se log hain yani, jo kam kaaj jo karte hain, unko bulake inki aapas mein meeting chal rahi hai. Wazir-e-aazam aur ye vo, to bhai ka agar raafta hota hai aap tak, bolo phauran vo ilaka chhor nikal lo bolo.* (And the people from this line, who do this work [anti-hijacking work] they have been called and there is a meeting going on. The prime minister and all that. So if there is contact with Brother, tell him to immediately leave the area.)

Latif: *Hmmm.* (Hmmm.)

Rauf: *Us taraf gaon ki taraf nikal, madarse ki taraf niklo fauran.* (Tell them to immediately rush to the village, then go to the madrassa.)

Latif: *Hmmm.* (Hmmm.)

Rauf: *Doosri ye hai ki yahan par media wale media mein khabrein aani chahiye thi ki jaanwar kitne hain. Uski khabar nahin aaee hai.* (Secondly, there should have been news in the media here about how many animals there are. There is no word on that.)

Latif: *Achcha.* (OK.)

Rauf: *Kaise bhi yeh khabar leak honi chahiye, mehnat jaanwaron ka hai. Yahan to saale chamaron ko pata bhi nahin hai, kisi ko hosh bhi nahin hai kuchch ho raha hai. Main ye to pata chale ki kitne jaanwar hain, phir vo shor machaenge.* (This news should be leaked anyhow. Over there these [expletive] don't know, no one knows if anything has happened at all. First let it be known how many animals there are, then everybody will make a noise.)

Latif: *Kuchch pata hai kitne?* (Do you know how many?)

Rauf: *Nahin ... yeh media wale bhi...abhi itna bataya ki abhi tak inhone khabar nahin di ki kaun hain aur kitne hain, bachche kitne, aurtein kitnee, sari khabrein daba ke baithe hain. Bola bilkul saamne hi nahin aa rahe. Inko media ko bahut door rakha hua bole inhone. To bhai se kaho ki media se kareeb ho jao andar se, andar mein hoega* phone *ka hisaab-kitaab, khud* media *se contact karo. Aur doosri cheez hai, teesri cheez yeh thi ki* deadline *ab tak nahin di hai inhone. Kafi der ho rahi hai.* Deadline *bolein, itna lamba kuchch nahin hota hai. Kaat-kaat ke likho, bolo,* Amritsar *mein hi bolna do-chaar tohfe de do unko.* (No. These media people ... even now they haven't reported how many there are, how many children, how many women, they are not saying anything. They [media] are nowhere close [to the plane]. They have been kept very far off. So tell Brother to make contact with the media from inside, there will be a phone arrangement inside. And the second thing is ... third thing is that they haven't given a deadline yet. It's getting very late. Tell them to give a deadline, all this delay shouldn't take place. Tell them to hack and give two or four gifts in Amritsar itself.)

Latif: *Hmmm.* (Hmmm.)

Rauf: *Tabhi to asar padega... Andar kya chal raha hai? Vaise yahan jo khabrein mili hain aur ye keh rahe hain humne bahut door rakha hua hai.* (That's how there will be some effect. What's going on inside? The information I have here is that we have kept it [the plane] very far off.)

Latif: *Hmmm.. chalo Allah malik hai, intezaar kar raha hoon. Raafta vagairah karne do phir.* (Well, Allah will take care. I am waiting. Let them contact.)

Rauf: *Haan, raafta karke bhi in baaton ka khas ...chhor devein ilaka, mulk ki sarhadon ko. Doosra yeh hai ki media se contact karo bolo.* (Yes, when there is contact, make sure of these things — leave the area, leave the country's boundaries, Secondly, tell them to contact the media.)

Latif: *Hmmm.* (Hmmm.)

Rauf: *Nahin hai unke paas koi number to, bolna aap do unka number varna aap do authorities ... Aap raafta karein media se.. Kuchch karein matlab.* (If they don't have the numbers [for the media], you give him the numbers. Or you contact the media. I mean, just do something.)

Latif: *Jee, jee, theek hai.* (Yes, Yes, all right.)

Rauf: *Media shor machaega na, usi ke upar hai sara kuchch.* (When the media will make a noise, everything depends on that.)

Latif: *Theek hai.* (OK.)

Rauf: *Theek hai, rakhoon phir? Khuda Hafiz.* (OK, shall I hang up then? May God help.

Latif then dialled another number, this time in Dubai, and related the whole story to a man called Furqan. Unknown to him, intelligence officials were listening in.

The intercepted conversation showed that the hijacking was being controlled by Rauf in Karachi, helped by Latif in Bombay; that the hijackers had the means to contact their accomplices outside the plane, but that Ibrahim Athar had not been able to do this so far in Amritsar. It indicates that they also had an informant who tipped them off on the meeting of the CMG — which had not been reported in the media by that time — and plans of an imminent commando raid. Rauf also wanted the hijackers to go immediately "towards the village, and then towards the madrassa" — a reference to the route to their destination. He called the hostages *jaanwar* (animals) and wanted Latif to convey to the hijackers that they should kill a few of them (give them a few gifts). Rauf had also been informed that the media was not being allowed into the Amritsar airport, and he wanted Ibrahim Athar to call journalists himself from inside the plane through a phone.

Inside the plane, this was a testing time. In the economy class cabin, Shankar, Bhola, Doctor and Burger started screaming at the passengers, asking them not to raise their heads or they would be killed immediately. The passengers did not realise where they were. All the windows were swiftly shut, and the four men grew very anxious. Shankar walked to one vacant row on the left, and sat down on the window seat. Then he slid up the window and looked hard, peering through his mask and still holding his gun. He wanted to be sure there was no suspicious movement on the tarmac. Then he spotted a packet of peanuts on the food table in front of him. He opened the packet, picked it up with the hand in which he held the grenade, used his other hand, holding the revolver, to pull up the mask right up to his forehead, and then emptied all the peanuts into his wide open mouth. For the first time, passengers sitting some seats away saw his face.

Passengers who wanted to go to the toilet started getting restless. Finally the hijackers asked people to raise their hands if they wanted to go. Just like in a classroom in school, Kollattu Ravikumar thought as he raised his hand. The 41-year-old merchant navy captain, who works for a United States-based company, was returning from a holiday in Nepal. Shankar walked forward and put a pistol on Ravikumar's head.

"*Kya chahiye?* (What do you want?)" he asked.

"I want to go to the toilet."

"No, you cannot go," Shankar snapped and took a close look at him. Then he started asking questions. "What is your name? Where are you from? Where do you work? Show me your identity card." Ravikumar's company identity card was in his hand baggage, so he took out his wallet and showed Shankar his voter identity card. Bhola walked up to the two men, and noticed Ravikumar's close-cropped hair.

"*Intelligence ke liye kaam karte ho?*" (Do you work for the intelligence?)

There was another captain who wanted to make sure the hijackers did not see his identity card. Captain Rajeev Raghavan of the Indian Army was returning from Kathmandu with his wife after their honeymoon. As the hijackers started questioning people closely, Capt. Raghavan walked briskly to the toilet, took out his identity card from his jeans pocket and hid it inside his clothes.

In the cockpit, Capt. Sharan was literally at the edge of his seat as he spoke on the radio after receiving another threat from Chief. It was 6:48 p.m. "As per them (hijackers), if there will be any movement ... first of all they will kill one of us of the cockpit crew and they will kill ten passengers whom they have already selected," he said. They hadn't selected the passengers yet, but Burger, Shankar and Bhola started doing that now. The three men walked down the aisle, looking hard at the men. They chose seven men and pulled them crudely holding the scruffs of their collars. The men, including Belgian national David Jansen, meekly followed as Burger took them to the business class.

"Sit!" he ordered.

The frightened men sat down, six of them taken without their blindfolds, and Burger kneeled down by the side to take out a ball of strong yellow nylon cord from his bag. He snapped it with his knife at several places, and then tied the hands of the seven men tightly at the back. They winced in pain, it hurt. The rope marks would not go away for weeks.

Daman Soni, the New Delhi businessman, and Chander Chhabra, the man who found the wad of currency notes in the departure lounge, were among the seven men. On Soni's right was another young man whose name he would learn much later — Ripan Katyal. The 25-year-old man from Gurgaon town adjoining New Delhi had got married to 22-year-old Rachna three weeks ago and was returning from his honeymoon in Kathmandu. Katyal was a fun-loving man, popular among his peers at the Jawaharlal Nehru Engineering College in Aurangabad, from where he graduated in electronic engineering in 1994 and later set up his own business. His wife looked up helplessly at Ripan as he was herded into the business class cabin, Burger pulling him as he clutched his yellow pullover. Ripan was originally scheduled to fly on 22 December, but he had called his father and told him he wanted to stay for two more days.

One of the seven men pleaded to Burger in a loud whisper: "I have to go to the bathroom, can I go to the bathroom now, please? You can tie me after that."

"No, shut up," Burger said.

"Please ... please. I can even use a bottle or something, right here."

On the tarmac, the fuel tanker was not ready, and to make matters worse, there were two phone calls made in quick succession to the Amritsar ATC. The first was from a man who identified himself as G.Lal, a joint secretary in the home ministry in New Delhi. He ordered the staff to immediately start refuelling. Minutes later, Cabinet Secretary Prabhat Kumar called, asking officials to delay refuelling for as long as possible. When a puzzled Kumar was told of the previous phone call, he said there was no such official in the ministry.

In the cockpit, Chief poked the gun harder into Capt. Sharan's neck, as he taxied the plane back and forth along the runway. Ibrahim Athar was getting furious now. *"Tel kyon nahin aa raha hai? Paanch minute mein tel chahiye.* (Why isn't the fuel coming? I need it in five minutes)" Chief snarled.

Capt. Sharan lunged for the radio: "They have only five minutes. Please send it fast. Please send it fast. Roger Sir, please send within five minutes otherwise they are going to blow (up) one of us. Please send it fast, immediately, otherwise one of us will be shot down." It was 7:05 p.m. Now Chief was accompanied inside the cockpit by Doctor.

A voice inside the Amritsar ATC tower across the tarmac responded quickly: "Immediately, Sir. As soon as they (oil tanker) will come. They will be immediately on site."

By claiming that a fuel tanker was not immediately available, Amritsar was trying its best to delay the hijackers, but officials in New Delhi were smug in the thought that the plane had nearly run out of fuel and could not take off again. The ATC told Sharan that his plane had arrived at a time when landings do not normally take place, and that the Indian Oil Company had been informed to send the fuel.

[32]

Two minutes later, Capt. Sharan said: "As per them, *'Agar kisi ne ustadi dikhane ki koshish ki to bhoon ke rakh denge.'* (If anyone tries to act smart, we will kill everyone). They have grenades in their hands and revolvers and AK47. Everything in their hand and we can see that. Roger."

Eight minutes later, at 7:15 p.m., both Capt. Sharan as well as Chief were running out of patience. The pilot shouted: "Why are you taking that much time? Guns are on our heads now." Minutes later, Chief asked him to turn the plane around once again on the runway. At 7:21, Capt. Sharan conveyed the hijacker's stern warning: "We have to see the (fuel) bowser. Once we make 180 degree. Roger. If he does not see the bowser he will kill us now."

A fuel tanker was ready by now with Punjab police commandos hidden in the vehicle waiting for instructions from the airport authorities. But the delay was too suspicious for Ibrahim Athar. His threat of harming passengers had so far had little effect, and he signalled to Doctor.

Doctor turned around and opened the cockpit door. The hijackers were furious now at the delay in refuelling. Doctor walked out, holding a sharp knife in his right hand, and stared hard at the passenger right in front of him — Ripan Katyal. Without a word, he pounced on Katyal like a frenzied maniac. As Katyal watched in icy, terrified silence, Doctor took two steps forward, coming right up to the bound and seated man. In a split second he took his arm half-way back and plunged the dagger near Katyal's left shoulder. With cold sweat on their foreheads, the other men heard the muted noise of the knife ripping through Katyal's body, then heard him cry out. Doctor slashed him again, this time by the side of his neck, and, like a maniac, dug his knife into Katyal's body several times. The young electrical engineer, tied to his seat, heaved loudly and his neck slumped to his left. His warm arm touched the right arm of Daman Soni; Soni drew away in terror. The men closest to him heard the gentle sound of the knife ripping through flesh and blood gurgling out of his neck. It flowed down his chest and shoulder, drenching his clothes and his seat. Then Doctor turned to another man sitting nearby — Satnam Singh, a farmer from Punjab — and took a wild swipe that slashed his jaw. Doctor stabbed Singh four times — once under his chin, twice on the sides of the face and once at the base of his neck. Singh passed out and slumped on his seat.

Shankar supported Katyal's body for a second as he toppled to one side. When he moved away, Shankar had blood on his fingers. He came to the kitchen area and the economy class and wiped two blood-dipped fingers on the side wall of the plane. It was an electrifying sight for the passengers who could see him: the fingers left two long red lines of blood. Doctor was more low-profile. He walked to a green curtain between the cockpit and the business class, and wiped his blood-laced knife, with which he had slashed the two men. The bloodletting over, Doctor stepped into the cockpit again and told Chief about what had happened. Chief put his gun on Capt. Sharan's head.

"Humne passengers ko marna shuroo kar diya hai" (We have started killing the passengers!), he announced in a cold, matter-of-fact tone. It was 7:23 p.m.

Capt. Sharan was back at the radio, shouting desperately after the sudden turn of events. "They are going to kill us any time. Please send the bowser. They have started killing us now. Where is oh ... Where is the bowser now? Please tell us ..."

Chief was determined, and he ordered Capt. Sharan to take off. "I will count up to thirty. If you do not take off by the time I finish, I will kill everybody."

"Pilot — one ... two ... three ... four ..."

Doctor stepped out again, and saw both Katyal and Singh still slumped on their seats, bathed in their own blood. He ran down the aisle to where Dr. Anita Joshi was sitting. He suddenly remembered their conversation some time ago. "Ma'am, are you the doctor?" he asked. Dr. Joshi said yes, got up and followed quietly. Then the hijacker shouted for the stewards to bring a first-aid kit. Senior Flight Purser Anil Sharma rushed with a small box. The other passengers watched, puzzled; none of them knew, and most of them would not know until a day later, about the incident. Dr. Joshi, who runs a nursing home in Nainital, was shocked as she saw the two men sprawled on their seats. "What did you do to them?" she cried out.

"It's all your government's fault," Doctor said and walked a few steps away. Then he turned back and said: "*Yeh bach jaega na?*" (He will survive, won't he?). Dr. Joshi did not say anything as she dressed the wounds of the men groaning and writhing in pain. There was a painkiller in the first-aid kit and Satnam Singh slowly gulped it down. Katyal was too senseless to have anything. His jugular vein seemed to have been sliced. Dr. Joshi suggested that Katyal be rushed to a hospital immediately — a request that was shrugged off — but even she knew that there was little that could be done. He was bleeding to death.

"Papa, *paani* (water) ... Papa, *paani* ... Papa, *paani*," Katyal moaned at regular intervals. It was obvious he was in excruciating pain and beginning to fade out. Behind him, Satnam Singh groaned similarly. Dr. Joshi wrapped a bandage on Satnam Singh's wounds, and then went back to her seat. When other passengers asked her what happened in the business class, she just shrugged her shoulders and said: "Nothing."

"Twenty-three ... twenty-four ... twenty-five ..." Chief had not stopped counting. When he reached twenty-seven, Flight Engineer Jaggia — grandfatherly, balding, portly and otherwise authoritative — sprang from his seat and put his palm on Chief's mouth, pleading with him to stop. Jaggia then kneeled down and held Chief's feet. "Please *ruk jaiye* (stop)," he said as he looked up.

As Jaggia stood up again, the sluggish-looking Chief pushed him away. The flight engineer's arm hit the fire-extinguisher. Then he kicked Jaggia with brute force above the ankle, a painful blow that would leave a scar even after a month. Pausing for only a second, Chief then banged Jaggia's right shoulder with the butt of his revolver and dragged him out of the cockpit to near the kitchen area, holding the stunned Jaggia by the scruff of his shirt. In the messy business class, Jaggia saw Ripan Katyal and Satnam Singh sprawled, their bodies soaked in blood. Shankar gently prodded a dagger into Jaggia's shoulder, staining his neck with blotches of blood. Jaggia was to wear that shirt for the rest of the journey.

Jaggia went inside, and Capt. Sharan understood from one look at his shirt that the hijackers were ruthless people who meant business. Now Chief was accompanied by Burger in the cockpit, and he started the count up to thirty once again. He put a gun to Jaggia's head. Now it was Capt. Sharan's turn to fall at Chief's feet. The blood-stained knife held to his throat, Jaggia mumbled what he had seen outside. The pilot turned to the radio set and bellowed: "He has already killed a passenger now. Why have you not responded? Now we have stopped. The bowser is not coming here. What is the problem?" It was 7:25 p.m.

Airport officials at Amritsar had a double dilemma on their hands. The hijackers refused to talk to them — this was understandable. But CMG honchos in New Delhi also didn't seem on talking terms. Of the few instructions Amritsar officials say they received from New Delhi, one call turned out to be a hoax, and the other — to try to immobilise the aircraft — came too late. In New Delhi, commandos were ordered to prepare for an operation only at 6:25 p.m., about hundred minutes after Capt. Sharan first reported the hijacking, and when they were ready to leave at 7:10 p.m. with their sophisticated gear, no negotiators were available and the ones asked to come were not on time. Officials still preferred to wait, because the rule book on hijacking said that negotiators must accompany commandos.

That lack of quick decision-making frittered away all the advantage Capt. Sharan had given Indian authorities by using his presence of mind and initiative to bring the aircraft to Amritsar, persuading a hardened hijack leader who did not want to land anywhere in India.

After nineteen difficult minutes spent waiting for fuel, and cajoling, persuading and failing to convince the two armed men, Capt. Sharan was back on the radio. Chief asked him to tell ATC that they had killed four and were now about to start killing the others. "They have killed four persons. They are starting killing everybody already and they will kill everybody now," he shouted.

What Capt. Sharan told ATC officials from the cockpit — under duress — also contributed to the confusion. He gave the impression to the airport officials that the plane had nearly run out of fuel when it landed in Amritsar, though it kept its engine running for more than forty minutes, that the hijackers had Kalashnikovs, and that they had killed four people and were ready to kill more. This stopped officials at Amritsar from sticking their necks out before a bunch of desperados — especially when little backing was available from New Delhi.

The fuel bowser miraculously appeared some distance away, but it was moving peculiarly. The driver had been told to block the runway, and, with misplaced enthusiasm, he started driving towards the cockpit at high speed to be able to block the runway from the front. Police commandos were also on the vehicle. In a normal refuelling, he would have driven towards the centre of the plane to park below the wings of the aircraft, in which the fuel tanks are located. When the ground control asked him to drive at normal speed to avoid suspicion, the driver screeched to a halt, then started moving slowly.

For Ibrahim Athar, watching the goings-on from inside the cockpit, the signs were too strong that police officials at Amritsar were planning something. He continued his upto-thirty count and prodded Capt. Sharan hard to leave. When Athar reached thirty, it would be the turn of Daman Soni, sitting tied next to Katyal. Sharan pleaded that he was in the middle of the runway and could not take off, but Chief seemed unstoppable and impossible to convince. He asked Sharan to take off immediately, even if he had to crash the aircraft.

The co-pilot shouted a parting message to ground controls: "We are taking off from our present position. We are taking off. We are all dying now. No bowser. We are going to take off from here."

By this time Chief had reached the count of twenty-seven, and the plane lunged forward from where it was standing, halfway through the runway with only about four thousand feet available to take-off, a nearly impossible task. As stunned officials watched from the control tower, the plane raced down the metalled runway, the end of its right wing narrowly missing a collision with the fuel tanker. As it neared the end, the flight engineer gave it full throttle power. Miraculously, the aircraft managed to lift off from the sheer end of the runway. Daman Soni took a deep breath. His face was awash in cold drops of sweat: if the plane had not taken off at that moment, it was his turn to be killed next.

About an hour later, the transport aircraft carrying commandos of the National Security Guards landed on the same runway.

In his silent prison cell in Jammu's Kot Bhalwal jail a few hundred kilometres to the north, Maulana Masood Azhar was rising from his evening namaz when the plane took off into the dark skies above Amritsar. The end of the holy month of Ramzan was getting closer; Eid was round the corner. He sat on folded thighs, rubbed his face with both his palms, and, with a sigh and some effort, got up. He walked across the room and picked up his radio transistor set, breaking the silent monotony of his prison cell with the screeches and burps and sputters of shortwave broadcasts. Finally, he managed to tune in to the local evening news at 7:30. The lead story was not about more killings in Kashmir. It was about the hijacking of an Indian Airlines passenger plane. The identity of the hijackers remained unknown, and Azhar would know much later that the man leading the hijackers was his own brother. Whoever those men were, they were as good as friends for many residents of Kot Bhalwal that evening. As word spread, prison inmates loudly cheered the hijacking and celebrated it with religious slogans. But Azhar remained silent, as always, not a hint of expression on his face.

Hundreds of kilometres to the east, in a small room in chilly Kathmandu, a small group of men also sat expressionless, poring over sheafs of papers and maps. In one corner of the room was a large, ancient-looking heater; the curtains were drawn, and five investigators sat facing each other across the cream-coloured wooden table, barely speaking a word. The senior man among the group, his hair gray and thick glasses resting on his nose, was taking a quick, hard glance at the list of passengers on board Flight 814, trying to identify who among them could be the hijackers. The passenger manifest had been divided into separate sheets, with the names of men, women and children divided on different pages. The bespectacled man put away the lists of the women and children. He struck off the names of the married couples, old people and names that sounded foreign. Then he ran his index finger down the men's page, reading slowly and very carefully, and stopped at one name.

"Sunny Ahmed Qazi. Hmmm," he said. This passenger had taken three economy class boarding cards, the tickets had three consecutive numbers, but the people in the group sat on different seats. The bespectacled official took a second to satisfy himself that his hunch was correct: the three economy class seats were in the front, middle and back. The official banged his finger on Qazi's name.

"I've got three here," he told his colleagues.

Within fifteen minutes, the spectacled man had prepared a list of nine possible hijackers. Now they would wait for further information to try and make out who the men were, and what they wanted.

[40]

Some time later at New Delhi's South Block, where government ministries are housed in a huge red sandstone building, External Affairs Minister Jaswant Singh was on a long distance call with a man he had come to know well over two years: the U.S. Deputy Secretary of State Strobe Talbott.

It was a macabre sight, as if the passenger cabin had been transformed into a tiny battlefield in the air after a bloody skirmish. Two men lay senseless, sprawled on their seats in tiny puddles of their own blood. Six others sat motionless and soaked in sweat and terror, their backs reclining gingerly against their seats. Ripan Katyal was still moaning for water, still calling out for his father, but his voice turned a few decibels feebler every time his trembling lips uttered those words : "Papa, *paani* ..." Every breath came with greater effort. His pullover was totally discoloured now, drenched in blood, and small rivulets of red made their way down his shoulder, down his arm, down his chest, down his waist to the cushioned seats. Not far away, Satnam Singh lay unconscious, part of his face splashed in red and slashed flesh visible beneath it.

In the cockpit, only vaguely aware of what had happened outside his door, Capt. Sharan made an ascent over Amritsar, and Chief ordered him again to go to Lahore — where officials had earlier turned the plane away. The flying time to Lahore is just over three minutes, but even that seemed such a long journey. There was hardly any fuel left in the Airbus — it would last just about eleven minutes. And Lahore had denied it landing permission once again. The Airbus hovered over Lahore, hoping to be allowed to land, but the airport was just an ocean of darkness, and landing there would be suicidal. All the lights along the runway had been switched off. The fuel remaining was now worth just a few minutes in air, and Chief did not want to return to Amritsar — the nearest airport — at any cost.

Capt. Sharan took a quick decision. He saw a brightly lit road adjacent to the airport, and decided to do the best thing possible under the precarious circumstances — crashland the plane. He began a swift descent. Inside the passenger cabin, people let out muffled shrieks of anguish as the plane started plummeting down the dark sky. Many had already given up on their lives, and thought the end had finally come. The huge Airbus coursed down at the speed of seven hundred feet per minute, and, within minutes, had readied an approach towards the road. The plane was about to land when, at a height of just 150 feet from the road, electricity ran down Capt. Sharan's spine. The road on which he was about to crash the plane was a very busy road, and there could have been more casualties on the ground than in the plane if he had gone ahead with the landing. Down below, there was an Iftaar party going on by the road, where dozens of people had assembled after their Ramzan fast. The decision must have taken a fraction of a second — he would not have thought of it then, but breaking into an Iftaar party with a planeload of two hundred uninvited guests was in any case a bad idea. He opened the power and pulled up. If he had continued at the same speed of descent for ten more seconds, there would have been disaster. Inside the passenger cabin, people were being tossed up and down and sideways as the plane swerved and plunged as if sliding up and down the slippery slopes of a mountain. The hijackers also seemed numbed by the killing uncertainty.

Capt. Sharan had thought he would crash the plane further ahead, but he suddenly turned lucky. The Lahore airport officials quickly switched on the runway lights, following it up with runway clearance. With one and a half minutes of fuel remaining, the aircraft had a bumpy landing on the 11,000-feet runway. There was a huge bang as the plane made the emergency landing. According to Indian time, it was 8:07 p.m. Armed commandos in green uniforms, several wearing long beards, moved in almost immediately to surround the aircraft. Chief had only one demand: the plane should refuel and quickly leave Pakistan. Airport officials had sealed the periphery of the airport. Ambulances streaked into the airport premises.

In New Delhi, Foreign Minister Jaswant Singh picked up the phone in his office and spoke to his counterpart, Pakistani Foreign Minister Abdul Sattar, for his help in ensuring the safety of the passengers. It was the first communication between the two foreign ministers since the 12 October military take-over in Pakistan. At the same time, Foreign Secretary Lalit Mansingh was on the phone with the U.S. ambassador in New Delhi, Richard Celeste, and Mark Sheehan, the special coordinator of the American government's counter-terrorism unit in Washington. Both promised help, and reportedly assured the Indian government that the plane would not be allowed to take off from Al Minhad.

Inside the plane, the hijackers were infuriated by an upstart passenger, Rajeev Ahuja. The New Delhi business-man was very uncomfortable with his blindfold. He twitched and shuffled in his seat in a front row, watched carefully by Doctor and Burger. He was making too many movements, and the two men became suspicious. Unable to take it any more, Ahuja took off the blindfold soon after the plane took off from Amritsar. Doctor took two measured steps towards him and said: *"Agar isko phir se nikala to tujh ko aage le jaunga aur bakiyon ki tarah maar doonga* (If you take this off again, I will take you to the front and kill you like I killed the others)." For most passengers, taking people 'to the front' — the business class where the seven passengers were tied up — would become a euphemism for slaughter for the rest of the journey.

As the plane stood parked on the Lahore runway, Ahuja's blindfold slipped off his face. Doctor rushed to him, pushed his head forward, tied his hands at the back with the cloth napkin and pushed him. They walked to the back row of the business class, where Ahuja stumbled on a seat with his hands tied at the back. *"Chaar ko maar diya hai, ab tujhko maar denge* (We have killed four, now we will kill you)," Doctor snarled at Ahuja.

The hijackers were edgy, apparently unsure what stance Pakistan's military regime would take. The Harkat-ul Mujahideen, which is believed to have planned the hijacking, is backed by the Pakistani government. But this terrifying odyssey was in international media glare. Pakistani authorities negotiated with the hijackers and decided to allow the plane to refuel. Pakistan's military regime also promised to fly Indian High Commissioner Satish Lambah to Lahore from Islamabad in an army helicopter, but the chopper was not ready to fly until after the plane left Pakistan, and Lambah cancelled the visit. As the bowser slowly pumped fuel into the aircraft's tanks, packets of food and bottles of water were brought in and distributed to several women and children. Capt. Sharan then requested Chief to let the wounded passengers and the women and children get off the plane. The hijacker agreed, and Capt. Sharan informed the control tower, but the authorities surprisingly declined.

Chief asked Capt. Sharan to take off immediately. There was still no clue about the identity of the hijackers. However, a spokesman of the army-led government of the Punjab province, where the plane had landed, later surprisingly claimed that it was impossible to understand the language the hijackers were speaking.

The hijackers continued their patrol inside the plane. *"Hum aapko maarna nahin chahte hain"* (We do not want to harm you), Doctor declared. *"Hamare bhai masoon hain aur Kashmir ki jailon mein band hain"* (Our brothers are under arrest in Indian jails though they are innocent).

At about 10:30 p.m. Indian Standard Time, the plane took off again, for an unknown destination. Once the plane was in the air and gaining height, Chief ordered the next stop: "Kabul Chalo!" The Lahore ATC provided the directions and flight level for Kabul, but Kabul control refused to give clearance to the aircraft, saying it had no night landing facilities and the landing would be unsafe. The airport at Kabul has been badly damaged by war and reportedly does not have any operational radar navigational equipment. Already several hours into an energy-sapping flight, it would have been very difficult for Capt. Sharan to make a night-time landing at Kabul, where the pilot must rely on his own eyesight. Capt. Sharan told Chief there were only a few places they could now head to: Muscat, Sharjah, Dubai or Abu Dhabi. Muscat, the capital of the Gulf country of Oman, was requested for a landing but the ATC refused permission. Chief was running out of time. He had to stop for the night and refuel before heading for his original destination, Afghanistan. He quickly opted for Dubai, and the plane nearly did an about-turn and cruised towards the United Arab Emirates (U.A.E.).

But minutes later, as the plane flew over the Dera Ismail Khan area, ATC officials in Kabul made contact with their counterparts in Lahore. The plane could land in Kandahar, they said. Chief asked Capt. Sharan brusquely to turn to Kandahar. But the pilot, who frequently commands flights to the U.A.E., said there was enough fuel only to reach Dubai. For the first time, he ignored an order from Chief.

Outside the cockpit door, Ripan Katyal was nearing his end. He was breathing with great difficulty, fading off into nothingness, his lips twitching slowly once in a long while, though he looked as if he slept peacefully wearing a covering of red parchment. A lot of blood on his clothes had clotted. His head hung to a side, and as he gently breathed, his body heaved a few centimetres and the left arm grazed by the arm of Daman Soni, tied next to him. It was too much of a sight for even the hard-boiled Doctor. He took off Katyal's blood-stained pullover and shirt, and threw them on the side near the bathroom. Then he threw two blankets belonging to passengers over Ripan Katyal and Satnam Singh.

Rajeev Ahuja, the eighth man on the killing line, shivered in his seat and waited for his death. He could see two people lying senseless on their seats. Satnam Singh lay with his mouth open and tongue sticking out. The blanket had slipped off Katyal's torso and he was barechested now, his body gored by Doctor's dagger. There seemed to be deep stab wounds all over his neck and chest.

The bound men were frightened and thirsty. When they had pleaded for water long enough, the hijackers asked an air hostess to bring a bottle. As the men opened their mouths wide, she poured water down the throats, enough for just a few gulps. She was too scared to give water to Katyal, now about to die and escape his misery.

Daman Soni made another request: he desperately wanted to go to the bathroom. Doctor refused. Then Chief stepped out for a moment, and asked his accomplices to take the men back to the economy class.

"*Nahin, main isko marunga*" (No, I'll kill him), Burger growled as he looked at Soni.

"Sir, please *peechhe jaane deejiye. Agar hum kuchch bhi karen, hamein shoot kar deejiyega*" (Please let us go to the back. If we do anything, just shoot us), Soni pleaded. He and the other men walked back to the aircraft, the yellow nylon ropes loose but still wound around their wrists, their faces ashen. Soni took just about ten seconds to use the toilet, as Bhola was guarding the rear and shouting for him to come out.

The plane was nearing Dubai, and it was not yet certain if the authorities there would allow them to land. The hijackers started warning passengers to obey orders, keep windows shut and to keep their heads low down. Shankar took off the pin of his grenade and screamed: "*Yeh* grenade *hai. Hum tees hazar foot par hain. Agar yeh phat gaya, koi nahin bachega!* (This is a grenade. We are flying at thirty thousand feet. If it goes off, no one will survive.)"

Inside the cockpit, Chief was more relaxed now. He told Capt. Sharan with a smirk: "*Dheere chaliye, aaram se chaliye, koi jaldi nahin hai. Hamein Hindustan ko millennium gift dena hai*" (Fly slowly, fly carefully, there is no hurry. We have to give India a millennium gift).

The hijackers had already wrecked Christmas Eve parties for a lot of people in the plane and in two countries; now they were heading for a third. Dubai's international airport was abuzz with journalists and photographers but it was otherwise functioning normally, with no sense of urgency.

Journalists kept sauntering in, several dressed in flamboyant party dresses, some looking like they had had a few drinks, others reeking of liquor. All the senior officials seemed in a huddle. Journalists ran after the first official they saw near the airport building, and all blurted out the same questions at the same time: Was the aircraft coming to Dubai? Would it be allowed to land? The official looked tense and did not slow down as he walked on hurriedly. "We have no information," he muttered.

In the prisoner plane, Ripan Katyal was now dead. He had died of excessive bleeding somewhere between Lahore and Dubai, unnoticed by even the men tied up next to him and uncared for by the men who killed him. More than a dozen rows behind him, his wife of three weeks, Rachna, sat unaware, shuffling in her seat anxiously and raising her head at frequent intervals to see if her husband had returned from where the hijackers took him. No one told her. No one had the heart to tell her, not even the hijackers.

In the cockpit, Capt. Sharan lobbied hard on the radio with the Air Traffic Control at Dubai. He said there was very little fuel on the aircraft, and there were wounded passengers and women and children on board. ATC mulled over the request and consulted authorities, but preparations had also been made at the airport for a possible forced landing. Fire engines and ambulances were on standby. Security was increased inside the airport, and more officials were deputed. The decision by the authorities came quickly: the aircraft would not land in Dubai and normal flights would not be disrupted. But it would be allowed to land at another airport on humanitarian grounds. This was turning out to be a long hopping flight. The cockpit crew prepared for their third landing, and soon touched down.

At the Dubai International Airport, meanwhile, a little hide-and-seek game continued for about an hour, when an official came and said the plane "will definitely, hundred per cent, not land in Dubai." He was right. The Airbus had already landed at the Al Minhad military base about thirty kilometres (eighteen miles) southeast of Dubai, located in the middle of a desert. Hordes of reporters and photographers raced out of the Dubai airport. Until officials told them, many did not know where Al Minhad was — or even what it was. Cars raced through the city's roads, and out of Dubai, driving for about an hour before they reached Al Minhad, a lonely base with nothing built near it. The official at Dubai's airport would have won full marks for the statement: The plane was not in Dubai and not in Al Ain, a city that follows the capital Abu Dhabi. It was in between.

Capt. Sharan would not have thought of it, but it was the night of the twenty-fourth, and he was in the U.A.E. according to his plan. Only, his wife and kids were not there, there was a stranger poking a gun in his neck, there was no opportunity for a shopping spree and he wasn't sure if he would live until Christmas Day.

Blue and red lights of police cars flashed in the heart of the desert. Most of the lights at the military airport had been switched off. A military helicopter hovered above the Indian Airlines plane, its lights off, its drone echoing across the dark sandy expanse. Officers stood outside the base and denied entry to the growing crowd of journalists. "Go home," one said. Behind him in the distance, the red beacons on the plane flickered to match the lights on police cars. Three ambulances and three empty police buses raced inside one after the other, followed by two jeeps carrying extendable metal ladders, and catering trucks loaded with pre-packed meals and bottles of water. Camera crews of state-run television also drove in. A coroner's vehicle stood waiting in the distance in the remote base.

Brigadier Atiq Juma of the U.A.E. army was meanwhile at the Air Traffic Control talking to the hijackers, trying to restrain them, and arranging a barter: sick patients, women and children in exchange for food and fuel. Brig. Juma told reporters that two of the hijackers were Sikhs — an assessment proved wrong later — and they spoke English with an Indian accent. The U.A.E. government would acknowledge nearly three weeks later, on 11 January, that an official in the airport control tower had glimpsed the hijackers from a distance and mistakenly believed they were wearing Sikh turbans.

Soon after, Crown Prince Khalifa bin Zayed al Nahyan, deputy supreme commander of the U.A.E. armed forces, himself walked into the control tower and took up the negotiation with Chief, assisted by Burger. According to reports, the U.A.E. government had received a telephone call from Talbott, who was following the hijacking crisis closely and had urged the U.A.E. government to assist the Indians.

In New Delhi's foggy, chilly night, relatives of the hostages poured into the international airport, waiting desperately for some word on the condition of their kin. Civil Aviation Minister Sharad Yadav and Minister of State Chaman Lal Gupta walked in one after the other to face the angry crowd. As the crowd grew raucous, Yadav stood on a chair and addressed the people, many of whom raised their fists and shouted abuses at the airport officials. Every word was drowned in the anxious cacophony.

Inside the plane, there was absolute silence. The blindfolds were in place; the passengers had their heads tucked between their legs. Burger shouted out: *"Koi mareez hai?"*

(Are there any patients here?) Others walked down the aisle, singling out women and children, and gesturing to them to get up. Not knowing they were being released, they meekly followed. Two elderly men were also asked to get up. Rajeev Ahuja, still tied up in the business class seat, saw his chance. Hungry to save his life, he pretended to be very sick, started wailing and put on a little hysterical act. He breathed hard, shuffled madly in his seat, hung his head apparently in extreme exhaustion, and told Burger: "*Mere dil mein chhed hai. main bahut beemar hoon. Doctor ne kaha hai ki dus barah saal se zyadah nahin jiyoonga*" (I have a hole in my heart, I am very sick, I am not going to live more than 10-12 years). Then he started making ugly sounds as if he was going to throw up on the seat, and coughed loudly and hoarsely.

Burger took a cold, hard look at Ahuja. "*Yeh theek hai*" (He's fine), he said. Ahuja could hear the loud shuffling of shoes and slippers in the background as twenty-five released passengers slowly walked out of the plane. Jittery and shaking with excitement, Ahuja continued to plead, holding Burger by the arms, nearly falling at his feet. "Please *chhor do* (leave me), for God's sake *chhor do. Maine kya kiya hai* (What have I done)? *Dekho main itna beemar hoon* (Look, I am so sick)," he said. Nothing worked, so he begged Burger to at least untie his hands from the back and tie them in the front.

"*Bahut dard ho raha hai*" (This is hurting so much), he said as he winced. That was enough provocation for Doctor, standing nearby. He pounced on Ahuja, violently pushed him back in his seat and nearly choked him by tying and tightening a black muffler around his neck.

"*Agar tune aur kuchch bola, ek baar bhi, to main ye muffler tere gale par baandh doonga aur isise tere pair baandh doonga.*

[51]

Tu hil bhi nahin paega" (If you say anything more one more time, just one more time, I will tie this muffler around your neck and feet, you won't even be able to move), he shouted, his eyes sizzling with anger. Then he paused for a second, and allowed Ahuja to go back to his seat.

As his mother walked away among the released passengers, a five-year-old boy slept peacefully on his seat. Chiragh Tyagi, who had a speech disorder, was left alone — his father had been separated from him and ordered to go to another seat, and his mother Pooja Tyagi was pushed out of the plane before she could realise her son was not with her.

Burger then walked up to Flight Purser Anil Sharma, who was now sitting in the passenger cabin with colleague Satheesh.

"Get up!" he said. They left their seats and followed him to the business class. Ripan Katyal's body had to be taken out of the aircraft.

"Lift him up. He's dead," Burger said, speaking in English. There were three hijackers in all surrounding Sharma and Satheesh, pointing their guns at the two horror-stricken men. Both of them hadn't even known that seven passengers had been taken to the front area and tied up — and that one was already dead. The five other men had been sent back to their seats, and the only other passenger there was Satnam Singh, who was groaning loudly.

They held Katyal's body, but could not lift it. It was too heavy. "Seat belt *bandha hoga"* (The seat belt must be tied), the hijacker told them. Sharma untied the seat belt, the nylon rope from his hands, and they gingerly lifted him, holding the body from both ends. Then they carried it past the business class seats, past the pantry area, and took it to the door. They placed the body at the top of the step ladder.

The police chief of Dubai and other officials stood some distance away. Three waiting doctors examined Katyal's body, his bare hairy chest visible in the dim lights, and examined his wounds.

"Get back quickly!" one of the hijackers, hidden from the officials waiting outside, screamed. Sharma and Satheesh were back.

Burger and Doctor walked towards Satnam Singh, the last remaining man among the seven they had brought. They held Satnam Singh by the hands and lifted him, walking forward as his limp figure followed senselessly. His wife had already got down with the other women. In minutes, Satnam Singh was on a wheelchair. He was with his wife. He was alive.

One task over, the U.A.E. authorities put in place an ambitious plan to end the hijacking. A crack team of army commandos was ordered to be on standby for a signal to storm the aircraft. The commandos took positions a safe distance away from the aircraft and the ATC indicated to Capt. Sharan that he needed to veer off the plane from the runway when he got the signal. The plan to rescue the hostages was elaborate, and even state-run radio broadcast news of the storming plan a short while after the plane left Dubai.

In the cockpit, Capt. Sharan and Jaggia planned to hoodwink the hijackers by having a 'reject take-off.' According to the plan, the plane would take off at about hundred nautical miles per hour, then accelerate to 145 nautical miles, when the pilot would suddenly pull back and descend, touch down on the runway, apply brakes and order evacuation, claiming falsely that there had been an engine fire. The chutes would come out and the hostages would run out of the aircraft, and simultaneously the commandos outside would storm it to eliminate the hijack-ers. Capt. Sharan informed the control tower using aviation language that Chief did not understand, and got a go-ahead from the control. But the plan could not be carried out as two hijackers remained inside the cockpit, looking over their shoulders.

The bowser was readied for refuelling the aircraft, and Flight Engineer Jaggia stepped out to assist the local engi-neers. After the refuelling was over, Jaggia adjusted the refuelling system immobiliser switch outside the aircraft to the Zero-Zero position, so that it would prevent future refuelling of the plane and possibly help end the hijacking. It was a crucial move.

The aircraft had spent five hours at Al Minhad, and Chief abruptly asked Capt. Sharan to take off. Chief told the cockpit crew they would fly to Kabul. *"Varna hum tayyare ko uda denge"* (Otherwise we will blow up the plane), he threatened. Then he asked the stewards to take out five life jackets for the five men.

Unable to match the pilots' sense of geography, Chief and his associates had assumed that the route to Kabul would be across an ocean.

DAY

2

===

In Kandahar, the hijackers are among friends
... they use fancy communication equipment
and announce their demands

Prime Minister Atal Behari Vajpayee woke up on Christmas Day, his birthday, grappling with a crisis that had got
out of his hands: he had to find a way to save the lives of
a planeload of passengers taken hostage by a group of
desperate men. Late in the night, he had asked his staff to
cancel the elaborate preparations his supporters had made
to celebrate his seventy-fifth birthday. Vajpayee's trouble-
shooters had not anticipated the sudden turn in the story
with the killing of Ripan Katyal, which became known
hours after his government's failure to stop the hijacked
plane in Amritsar. Despite a promise not to let the aircraft
take off from Al Minhad, the United States had not been
able to help New Delhi end the hijacking. And the hijackers
were now set to leave for Kandahar, headquarters of the

Taliban regime that controls about ninety per cent of Afghanistan. India would now have to deal with a regime with which it had no diplomatic relations, which it had for years identified as one of the fountainheads, along with Pakistan, of the terrorist campaign in Kashmir. Vajpayee was looking for a lot of answers. He also had a lot to answer for.

At the desert military base of Al Minhad in the U.A.E., the cockpit crew, extremely tired and emotionally drained by the horrors they had witnessed outside their cockpit door, embarked on yet another flight at the whim of their captors. Their Indian Airlines uniforms — white shirts and navy blue trousers — were dirty and smelling, their hair dishevelled, their eyelids drooping with fatigue, but more than that was the chilling realisation that they were so close to death every minute — the most stark reminder was the blotches of Ripan Katyal's blood that Flight Engineer Jaggia had on his shirt. The plane had already taken off and landed four times each, and Capt. Sharan had long crossed the international safety regulations that prohibit a pilot from flying more than seven hours continuously. It was nearly five in the morning according to local time when the plane took off from the Al Minhad airport, refuelled with more than 30,000 litres of aviation turbine fuel. There were two armed hijackers still inside the cockpit. Forced by Chief, Capt. Sharan made another attempt to seek landing permission at Kabul, which suggested he land at Kandahar. According to Taliban officials, Indian embassy officials in Islamabad had, meanwhile, got in touch with the Afghanistan embassy and requested the Taliban to allow the plane to land in Kandahar. It was a little after 8 a.m. local time that the plane touched down on the battered, wind-swept runway at Kandahar where shells have punched holes in the tarmac in years of fighting between armed rival groups. The airport consisted of a single landing strip and a run-down terminal building on the barren plains outside the city. The runway was flanked by bleak, cloud-kissed mountains. Taliban soldiers in long beards and shalwar kameezes dotted the tarmac, several armed with Kalashnikov rifles. A few hundred metres away, Taliban flags fluttered along a semi-circular column, a few white domes of mosques looming in the background. But the passengers could see neither the scenic beauty of the place they had landed in, nor experience the fear and uncertainty of arriving in an alien country with seemingly ruthless rulers. The windows were shut, the blindfolds were on and the passengers again had their heads on their knees.

Were they not trapped helplessly inside a huge Airbus, the visit to Kandahar, the second largest city in Afghanistan 320 miles southwest of the capital Kabul, could have been something to tell curious listeners about. It could sound like a journey to another, alien world. Believed to have been founded by the Greek emperor Alexander himself, the city was the capital of the kingdom of Afghanistan between 1848 and 1873, and was occupied twice by the British in the Afghan wars. It was the main military base of the erstwhile Soviet Union during the prolonged Afghan War in the 1980s. It is now the most important trade centre in war-torn Afghanistan, and the region's biggest market for sheep, cotton, grain and dried fruit. It was also associated with Indian history and mythology. Kandahar was the kingdom ruled by the scheming gambler uncle of the Kaurav rulers, Shakuni, and centuries later, the western-most outpost of the massive kingdom of Mughal emperor King Akbar.

But as the plane slowed down on the runway on the morning of 25 December, the only link that Kandahar seemed to have with India was of the terror spawned by five ruthless men. A phalanx of Toyota pickup trucks appeared in the distance, and stopped a few hundred feet away from the Airbus. Co-pilot Rajinder Kumar Goud was on the radio transmitter with the ATC, and the control directed the crew to follow a white Pajero to the taxi track about five hundred metres from the airport terminal. As the aircraft came to a halt, the vehicle drew up closer. Chief asked the crew to step out of the cockpit, and for the next fifteen minutes, spoke through the pilot's window with a Taliban official who had come in the vehicle.

If his main accomplice in Mumbai is to be believed, Ibrahim Athar was not talking to absolute strangers as he peered out of the window. Several days ago, Athar had told Abdul Latif — his key associate in Mumbai — that he had already contacted Taliban leaders in Kabul, including a wazir, or government minister, to inform them of the hijacking plan and to seek their approval. As Latif would tell investigators later, Abdul Jabbar, an activist of the Harkat-ul Mujahideen in Pakistan, was the intermediary between the hijackers and the Taliban before 24 December. After refuelling at Lahore, Kabul was the intended destination for the hijackers but the three-hour flight delay threw the plan into disarray and the long wait at Amritsar made a night escape to Afghanistan impossible. Despite the possibility of a very difficult landing late in the night, Kabul had offered the hijackers refuge after an initial denial when the plane took off from Lahore. For the remaining part of Saturday, the hijackers would make several more attempts to go to Kabul — where they hoped their friends would be waiting.

The Taliban leadership was swift to realise that the hijacked plane had arrived like a blessing in the holy month of Ramzan — it could give them the voice to speak with the outside world that had shunned them for years. It was time for some PR.

The hijackers asked the three crew members to step out and sit with the passengers. But before Capt. Sharan and Jaggia stepped out, they were asked to explain the working of the radio transmitters and other communication gadgets inside.

According to descriptions from crew members and passengers, the hijackers had sophisticated communication equipment with which they were giving and receiving instructions. Militant groups like the Harkat-ul Mujahideen and the Lashkar-e-Toiba are known to possess communication gadgets that are as good as the best in the world, and even better than the armies of many countries. One of the most important gadgets for the guerillas is a tiny radio set manufactured by companies like Icon, Yasu and Motorola which has a drooping antenna that varies from eighteen inches to upto five feet in length. The sets are so powerful that militants hiding in trenches near the Line of Control in Jammu & Kashmir can communicate easily with their accomplices in Islamabad. Bhola held a similar radio set the size of a cellular telephone with a drooping antenna that was shiny black in colour and at least two feet long. The hijackers also held a black Iridium satellite telephone. Some hostages who were allowed movement inside the plane and got close to the hijackers saw them dialling numbers on this phone.

Chief asked to be left alone, promising to summon the crew whenever he wanted, and switched on the radio set to open the first direct conversation with Kandahar ground control. Capt. Sharan would be called several times over the next several days to adjust volume or radio frequency, but Chief never held discussions in his presence. Jaggia would be asked frequently to attend to problems with the air conditioning, electrical fuses, lighting, servicing of water and the auxilliary power unit.

After delicate moments in Amritsar and Al Minhad when the plane could be stormed and his plan could go awry, Chief was now completely on his own. He had direct access to the Taliban inside the closed doors of the cockpit; there was also a small door in the cockpit floor that he opened every time he wanted something. The first consignment to arrive was of food and water. A small group of Taliban soldiers drove up in a Toyota truck with supplies packed in huge plastic bags and positioned themselves right under the cockpit of the aircraft. Chief then ordered his associates to open the hatch, and they lugged up the rations. There were apples — some with grass stuck on them, as if they had just been plucked from trees — oranges and packets of biscuits. When the food was about to be distributed, Chief stepped out of the cabin and told some passengers in the front rows: "*Main aapko udaas nahin dekhna chahta hoon. Mujhe aapke chehron par muskurahat chahiye*" (I don't want you to be glum. I want a smile on your faces). This would be among his rare, once-a-day interactions with the passengers. As the food reached passengers and they gently removed their blindfolds to eat, a chilling realisation set in, row after row after row. The biscuit packets had things written in Urdu. They were in an Islamic country. For the first time after the five men shocked them with their guns and threats, many passengers realised that they were not in India. Trapped in the plane with its windows shut and their eyes closed, there had been no Amritsar for the passengers, no Lahore, no Dubai. For them, it was just a rollercoaster journey in the skies that included landings at three unknown places, with the plane swerving and plunging occasionally as they sat like statues in their seats, with death hovering over their heads.

One woman among the passengers had no inkling that death had touched her from so close. Rachna Katyal, wife — now widow — of Ripan Katyal, sat silently, sometimes dozing off, then waking up and looking around anxiously. Then she broke into tears, crying for a long time as co-passenger Ipsita Biswal Menon, sitting next to her, tried to console her, telling her that Ripan had been released. She had not seen her husband for more than eleven hours now. She had barely got a glimpse of him as he was being pushed to the forward cabin. At Al Minhad, with a dupatta wrapped around herself, she had obeyed the hijackers and kept her head bowed, hearing the shuffling of feet and the sound of people walking in the aisle. She later asked Dr. Anita Joshi, who had attended to her husband in his dying hours, whether she knew what the hijackers had done to him. The doctor said she did not. When the waiting became too much and too painful, she gathered the courage and asked Doctor as he passed by her seat. "*Pata nahin mere husband kahan hain*" (I don't know where my husband is), she said softly. Doctor — who had killed her husband — paused for a moment and said: "*Vo Dubai mein utar gaye. Vo ghar pahunch jaenge*" (He got off in Dubai. He will reach home).

Ripan had not reached home. Unaware of their son's death, his parents stood waiting at the New Delhi airport with a large number of relatives, like other anxious families around them. Across the lounge, on large television screens, networks were reporting the death of one passenger. Shockwaves ran through the lounge. A distraught Ram Chameli, whose son and daughter-in-law were on board, started shouting, and threatened to immolate herself at the

[61]

airport if her children were not released. A short while later, a television network identified the dead man as Ripan Katyal. As word reached them on their seats across the lounge, Ripan's parents collapsed, wailing loudly, staring in anger and disbelief, their eyes clouded with tears, their arms holding on to their son's young cousins for support. Ripan's father Chandra Mohan Katyal apparently suffered a minor heart attack and was rushed to a hospital where he waited and wailed for his dead son.

Across the city, at his expansive residence, Prime Minister Vajpayee started gauging the opinion of senior colleagues to seek a way out of the biggest crisis for his government after the Kargil war with Pakistan. Views were divided. While some ministers wanted the government to take the difficult line of not negotiating with the hijackers at any cost, others cautioned that such an approach could have serious repercussions. Personalities also clashed. Foreign Minister Jaswant Singh was calling the shots along with senior bureaucrats in the Crisis Management Centre, leaving out two senior ministers — Home Minister Lal Krishna Advani, number two after Vajpayee in the Cabinet and an advocate of tough action against terrorists, and Defence Minister George Fernandes. The government's handling of the situation in Amritsar had provoked ridicule from several senior army officers, who pointed out that military commandos could have overpowered the hijackers in Amritsar. But Fernandes was personally hurt over being sidelined — he retreated to the North-east for three days and kept himself aloof from the crisis management.

Nearly 1,400 kilometres (840 miles) south of the hurly-burly of South Block corridors, Abdul Latif had a busy day ahead of him in Mumbai. Clean-shaven and wearing a T-shirt and jeans, he stepped out of his flat in the traffic-clogged Behrambagh neighbourhood in the Jogeshwari area, crammed by thousands of small houses, shops and slum clusters and overrun by armies of noisy vehicles. There was a phone booth nearby, and he knew very well the young Sheikh brothers — Rafiq, Javed and Muzaffar — who owned it. Most of his phone bills would come from calls to Karachi, and he was dialling one of the same numbers today. Latif was speaking in Urdu but he mentioned the words 'hijack' and 'hostage' more than once in his conversation. Indian officials believe that the voice at the other end belonged to Karachi-based Abdul Rauf, younger brother of both Maulana Masood Azhar and Ibrahim Athar.

As Latif spoke, another man standing nearby listened carefully. Some minutes later, Latif hung up and walked through crowded bylanes to a nearby mosque for prayers. The second man quickly walked away and made a local call from another booth.

"Crime Branch, Mumbai Police," said a voice at the other end.

At about the same time in New Delhi, it was another man making another call. The phone rang in the Air Traffic Control tower at the Indira Gandhi International Airport. "*Main* Islamic Salvation Front *se bol raha hoon*" (I am calling from the Islamic Salvation Front), the anonymous caller said. The confused official at the tower listened as the caller said he wanted to say something about the hijacking. Chaman Lal Gupta, state minister for civil aviation, took the receiver. The caller declared the group's demand to the government: if the passengers were to be freed, three mujahids (religious fighters) would have to be freed from Indian prisons. Two names were clear: Maulana Masood

Azhar and Mushtaq Ahmed Zargar. Gupta did not catch the third name properly — it sounded like Ahmad Omar Syed Sheikh — and the caller quickly disconnected the phone. Within the hour, Gupta told journalists about that call, and by the end of the day, he had been reprimanded by the prime minister as well as Foreign Minister Jaswant Singh for announcing it prematurely. The ATC was receiving hundreds of calls each hour, with ordinary people registering their anger, complaints, frustration, suggestions — anything that they felt, on the hijacking. Several callers suggested that the hijackers be fed poisoned food; others wanted Indian commandos to storm the plane; some wanted Indian soldiers to attack Kandahar. So officials promptly declared the call was a hoax. Without mentioning the purported demand, Vajpayee took a tough stand against the hijackers. In a statement distributed to reporters outside his residence by his press secretary, Vajpayee said: "My government will not bend before such a show of terror ... This hijacking is an act of terrorism by desperate men who have no respect for human lives and human rights. It has brought home with full impact the horror of terrorism that the country faces."

Intelligence officials, meanwhile, wracked their brains on whether the caller could be linked to the hijack. Masood Azhar was a name that came ringing back — old Kashmir hands had not forgotten him despite his long years in oblivion after his arrest. The other man — militant leader Zargar — was the terror-monger of Srinagar before his arrest, notorious for a spate of killings of political activists, policemen and soldiers. But, if it did exist, what was the Islamic Salvation Front?

According to investigators in India and other countries such as the United States which are facing a growing threat from Islamic fundamentalist groups, Pakistan's Inter Services Intelligence agency arms and funds a string of militant outfits like Maulana Masood Azhar's Harkat-ul Mujahideen (previously known as the Harkat-ul Ansar, it changed its name after the US put it on its list of international terrorist organisations), the Lashkar-e-Toiba, the Al Badr, and Osama Bin Laden's Al Qaeda. All these organisations are members of Bin Laden's International Islamic Front, also called the International Islamic Salvation Front, the aim of which is to wage a religious war against the US and Israel. It is impossible to tell if the unidentified caller was linked to Bin Laden's front, but the names of Azhar, Zargar and Sheikh would soon return to haunt the hijacking crisis. Interestingly, Bin Laden issued a statement later the same day, saying that India, the US and Russia were the enemies of Islam, and that the jehad in Kashmir would continue.

As the day passed, officials in India assessed the impact that the Taliban's special relations with Pakistan would have on the way that regime handled the hijacked plane, and tried to understand the web of Afghan politics.

Since September 1996, Afghanistan has had two power centres. Kabul is the administrative capital and the seat of the council of ministers headed by Mullah Mohammad Rabbani. Kandahar is the spiritual capital where Mullah Mohammad Omar, the all-powerful Amir of the Taliban — and reportedly one of the three fathers-in-law of Osama Bin Laden — heads his 30-member Shoora or consultative council. The Amir, who lost one eye while fighting Soviet troops, would have a key background role to play in the hijacking crisis. The Amir grew up in village Singsar in the Mewand district near Kandahar. Mewand is a holy and historic place for the Pakhtuns of Afghanistan. Afghan historians say that it was here that the Pakhtuns defeated the advancing British troops. Since the Amir belongs to the legendary Mewand district, the simple, God-fearing and proud Pakhtuns revere him and follow his commands blindly. But the Amir is a man with almost no exposure to the world outside Kandahar and its neighbourhood.

It was not known, therefore, whether the Amir and his Shoora, part of a Taliban-run government that is recognised by only three countries in the world, would take a larger view of the hijack drama and attempt to build new bridges with India's government — or if they would follow a myopic pro-Pakistan policy.

All appointments in the Kabul-based administration and all policy decisions are made by the Amir in consultation with the Shoora.

In Afghanistan, the Taliban overran ninety per cent of the country's territory and drove out the Tadjik-dominated Burhanuddin Rabbani government. The Taliban administration has since had to depend on the large-scale deputation of Pakhtun officers from Pakistan's North-West Frontier Province and Balochistan to run the administration. This has resulted in a substantial presence of Pakhtun civil servants of Pakistan in different government departments, including the intelligence agency, airport security and the Kandahar airport control tower.

It would soon become clear that the Harkat-ul Mujahideen, which is strongly backed by the Pakistani government, had planned the hijacking. Ibrahim Athar had sought help on the hijacking from a member of the Shoora, but even otherwise it was clear that the Taliban would have little choice apart from subtly backing the hostage-taking — Mullah Omar's regime was too dependent on Pakistan for money, rations, arms, ammunition and manpower for running the administration to stand up to Islamabad.

Chief was in a hurry, and he was irritated. More than twenty-four hours after he took over the aircraft, he had not reached Kabul, the destination he had set out for. For some reason, he kept insisting on going to Kabul — Kandahar was only second best. He opened the cockpit door and summoned Jaggia. Chief wanted the aircraft to be refuelled and then they would take off for the Afghan capital.

"*Usme* major repair *chahiye*" (It needs major repairs), Jaggia told him. The flight engineer's clever little trick of the previous night with the refuelling immobiliser switch seemed to be working. The change in the position of the switch remained undetected, and finally Chief realised that the rest of his plan would have to be executed in Kandahar, instead of Kabul. Still he asked Jaggia to go back to his seat, and switched on the radio set. Against Jaggia's wishes, he asked ground control to have local engineers refuel the plane, but they failed.

Soon after, he summoned Doctor. They were going to step out of the plane for the first time after the operation began. Masks in place, they opened the hatch door on the floor of the cockpit and stepped down an extendable metal ladder. It was a windy afternoon. Taliban soldiers watched silently from the distance, their loose dresses filled with the wind, their beards billowing in the air. Chief and Doctor walked down from the plane.

Some distance away, a man in a flowing dress with small twinkling eyes and a long beard, wearing rectangular-framed spectacles, was waiting for them. This was Mullah Wakil Ahmad Muttawakil, the foreign minister, who would become the genial face of the Taliban for the international media during the hijacking crisis. Muttawakil was new to his job — before 27 October 1999, he was just the media spokesman for the Amir, and the hijacked plane offered him a huge opportunity to prove himself before the Shoora. Muttawakil had now become one of the most important members of the council of ministers. He had joined the core quartet of Mullah Rabbani, the premier, Mullah Mohammad Hasan Akhund, his deputy and trusted adviser, Mullah Abdur Razzaq, the interior minister and Mullah Qudratullah Akhund, the minister for information and culture.

According to Muttawakil, Ibrahim Athar introduced himself as "Ibrahim, brother of Maulana Masood Azhar." Doctor did not identify himself. Azhar himself was a known figure in Taliban circles, and this was the first and last time that Chief's identity as his brother was made public by the Taliban. Days later, Maulana Masood, unaware that Muttawakil had identified his brother by name while he was behind bars, would disown Ibrahim and say that he did not know who the hijackers were and that he had no relation with them.

The Taliban did not want to be seen as allying with the hijackers and told journalists they had suggested the hijackers leave Afghanistan. Chief, however, had other views. Though handicapped by the technical problem in refuelling the aircraft, he told Muttawakil that they would land in Kabul if forced to leave the Kandahar airport. If that was also denied, they would crash or blow up the plane — but they would not leave Afghanistan, he reportedly said. Then Chief requested for political asylum. That would be difficult, he was told.

Finally, Chief asked Muttawakil to convey to India his first demand: the government should free Maulana Masood

Azhar, and along with him several other militants lodged in prisons in Kashmir.

Looking back, Chief would probably realise that Muttawakil's statement identifying him became the weakest link in a meticulous, perfectly-planned operation. Muttawakil remained closetted with the two hijackers for some time, and then they returned to the plane. Muttawakil was then occupied with telephone interviews to some of the world's biggest news organisations as he became the voice of the Taliban in the hostage drama.

Through its representative in New York, the Taliban soon passed on the demand to the United Nations, and demanded the UN negotiate with the hijackers. "We have conveyed their demand to the UN. It is up to the UN to intervene and end this. The Taliban will not mediate," he declared in Pashtu in one of his interviews conducted on a satellite phone.

Within hours, it was announced that the Islamabad-based UN official Erick du Mul would fly to Kandahar to negotiate with the hijackers. Apparently in preparation for his visit, bearded Taliban troops wearing black turbans encircled the aircraft. The airport was sealed.

In New Delhi, members of the Crisis Management Group went into a tizzy as soon as they heard of the demand formally made by the hijackers. It was already chaotic in the control room, with four telephone hotlines ringing nonstop, unshaven officials darting in and out of rooms and the fax machine churning out metres of urgent and confidential messages. In the corner was a television set on which news bulletins were being constantly monitored; one senior official also sometimes took time off to watch India's cricket tour in Australia! The demands showed that the hijackers were on a serious mission, and resolution of the crisis could take days. Stress levels were shooting up inside the room. More cigarettes were smoked, more black coffee ordered. Sometimes the officials snapped at each other. Ministers also walked in, spending hours in deliberations. Intelligence officials were asked to find out all about the people whose release had been demanded by the hijackers. In the rush, the anonymous call in the morning at the control tower was forgotten, though the man purportedly from the Islamic Salvation Front had also demanded that Maulana Masood Azhar be freed.

Across the border to the east in Kathmandu, authorities were still trying to overcome the shock of the previous evening's hijack, only the second in Nepal's 50-year aviation history and the first of an international flight. The government suspended the entire staff who were on duty at the time. The police in tight blue uniforms closed the Kathmandu airport to visitors, and the airport authorities refused to talk to journalists about how five men made it past the security checks with weapons. The tourism and civil aviation minister, Narayan Singh Pun, said the government had received warnings of possible attacks on the airport. The source is believed to be a blanket caution from the US in September of a possible attack on airports in the region by people linked to Osama Bin Laden. Indian Airlines cancelled all its flights to the Tribhuvan International Airport, and later suspended flights altogether. At the airport, there was a semblance of strictness — officials stopped issuing visitors' passes, and only people with tickets were allowed through the gates. Pun ordered temporary closure of all shops running on contract in the airport building. These included a money changer, a duty-free shop, a restaurant and two retail outlets for food and beverages in the departure lounge. The airport has been undergoing renovation since 1997, and some officials feared that the unrestricted access to unauthorised people within the complex could be linked to the smuggling of arms. But government officials also tried to deflect part of the blame for the hijacking, saying it was possible the weapons were on board the plane when it arrived from New Delhi.

In New Delhi, Captain R.N. Singh, a veteran pilot and also the general manager of Indian Airlines for its northern region, was taking off in an Airbus 320 from the runway at the Indira Gandhi International Airport. Sitting silently on a front seat was Civil Aviation Minister Sharad Yadav, who had been assigned the task of bringing back the released passengers, the injured Satnam Singh and the body of Ripan Katyal.

At Kandahar, the aircraft stood parked, its shutters drawn, its doors closed, with no way of knowing what was going on inside it. Chief was back in the cockpit, and the other four men took up positions some distance away from each other in the aisle. Bhola was shouting out: "*Kisi ke paas batteries hain?*" (Does anyone have batteries?) It seemed he wanted them for his communication set.

The weather forecast for Saturday was a high of eighteen degrees Celsius and a low of minus ten degrees. The consolation was that passengers could sit in a more relaxed position. For the unbearably hungry, there were peanuts and some fruits, and tea bags were distributed for passengers to have black tea. Gradually, the blindfolds started to come off. The passengers could turn to those next to them and talk in low voices. People did not have to beg to go to the toilet, the hijackers just called out the seat numbers. The hijackers had stopped slapping and kicking people. The aircraft was drowned in the first relaxed murmurs since it was gripped by terror on 24 December.

Burger played out the first round of the complex psychological games the hijackers had planned for the hostages, keeping them teetering between hope, fear and desperation. He made an unexpected announcement: *"Aap sabke liye khushkhabri hai, aaj raat nau baje tak aap sab chhor diye jaenge"* (There is good news, we'll release you by nine tonight).

"Humne Hindustan ki sarkar se kaha hai ki aap mein se dus-dus ke badle mein hamare ek saathi ko chhor de" (We have asked them to release one of our men for ten passengers each).

Suddenly things seemed to be getting better. For the desperate passengers who had lost all hope and were confined to their seats with cramps in their bodies, this was like a grand Christmas party: Food, lugged up the cockpit opening, was brought to the economy class after the hijackers had kept their share. It was a huge black plastic bag, similar to a trash bag, that contained servings of plain rice packed in silver foil. Passengers were given one plastic glass each, which they were asked not to throw away.

"Ramzan hai, sare restaurant *band hain"* (It's Ramzan time, all restaurants are closed), Burger said almost apologetically to explain the frugal dinner. Many people did not want to eat because the killing uncertainty had taken away their hunger. Others had more practical reasons: if they ate more, they would have to go to the toilet, which was beginning to stink badly.

Confined far too long in the same place, more or less the same position, the passengers were beginning to suffer from cramps and severe body ache, apart from stress and high blood pressure. But the agony of some passengers was much worse. 45-year-old Anil Khurana from New Delhi, who had come to Kathmandu on a business trip with his cousin Sanjive Sharma, was a severe diabetic who had to take two injections of insulin each day to keep his condition under control. Khurana took one injection before the flight took off from Kathmandu the day before, and would have taken the second one on reaching home. Now, his injections were inside the checked-in baggage in the luggage hold at the bottom of the aircraft, and his condition was worsening. He began to have convulsions, extreme dizziness and nausea, and needed to go to the toilet frequently. Chief first asked Dr. Anita Joshi to examine Khurana. Dr. Joshi gave Khurana some medicine, but with few medical supplies in the little first aid box, the patient's condition was beyond her now. Finally, the hijackers released him for a while to be taken to the local military hospital under the guard of Taliban soldiers. At about 9 p.m. local time, Chief was on the radio set again, asking the ground control to send Khurana back to the plane. About thirty minutes later, he walked in.

Almost at the same time, the Airbus 320 commanded by Capt. R.N. Singh started its descent over the New Delhi airport carrying one coffin and twenty-six passengers. Minister Sharad Yadav was back, delayed for hours in Dubai because the release of Ripan Katyal's body was caught up in bureaucratic formalities and the minister insisted he would not leave without taking the body. There were thirteen women and eleven children. As they landed, throngs of journalists and camerapersons at the airport erupted into chaos. The police whisked away batches of the passengers in waiting cars, the anxious drivers often pushing past crowds of reporters angry at not being allowed to talk to the hostages. Yadav spoke to the reporters and said there were six hijackers. Earlier in the evening, Foreign

Minister Jaswant Singh had said there were indications that the hijackers were seven in number.

Perhaps encouraged by the planned visit of the UN official to Kandahar, Jaswant Singh sounded optimistic: "I expect developments to take shape sometime tomorrow morning," he told journalists.

DAY

3

==

One man's release is another man's cremation, the passengers
are close to a nervous breakdown ... and the hijackers fortify
themselves with more arms, as the Taliban watch

Maulana Masood Azhar woke up on a chilly morning
in Jammu's Kot Bhalwal jail, unaware of everything that
had happened in Kandahar the evening before. He had
slept early after his dinner and namaaz on Saturday, a day
spent in hope and despair. The local radio station had reported that the Islamic Salvation Front had asked for his
release along with two others, but it was not certain if the
demand was authentic. Before going to bed, he had tuned
to the news on the Jammu radio station, but there were few
updates available from Kandahar. He got up from his bed,
had a quick wash, and in an hour got ready for more
prayers. Then a sentry walked up to him with his Urdu
daily. As he spread the front page before him, he saw his
name. He read the main story and related stories quickly,

watched by a prison official who had already heard his name on the news. As one would have expected, Azhar did not break into celebration, and did not betray any sign of being excited at the prospect of release. The officer stepped forward and mentioned the hijackers' demand to him. Now Azhar smiled weakly for a second.

"*Dekhiye khuda kya karta hai*" (Let's see what khuda does), he said. Then he added: "*Main baizzat jana chahta hoon*" (I want to go out with dignity).

Soon after, Azhar picked up his bag of clothes and walked slowly across the prison compound as he was shifted from his barracks to another one. He would now be alone, and guarded round the clock. Security was stepped up around the prison. Meanwhile, in Srinagar, dozens of extra policemen had already been deployed outside the Central Jail, where Mushtaq Ahmed Zargar was lodged.

Across the border, in Pakistan, Azhar's father Allah Baksh Sabir had already become a celebrity. Journalists were beginning to reach his home in Bahawalpur in eastern Punjab state, asking questions about Masood Azhar and Ibrahim Athar. Sabir denied his younger son was involved, saying he was in Saudi Arabia performing the Islamic pilgrimage known as Umra. It was not known whether the younger son had actually set out from home claiming he was headed for a pilgrimage, or whether his father was protecting him. "We are very worried about these reports, but I don't believe it is my son. He called from Saudi Arabia to ask about my health," Sabir said. "We have nothing to do with the hijacking. We condemn this and feel sorry for the people on the plane," he was quoted as saying in Urdu in published reports. "I pray for the lives of the passengers. May God protect them from every harm."

In the plane, the hostages had had breakfast. It consisted of omelettes, fruits and juice, and it came with a fresh stock of water. The passengers had eaten in their stuffy, closed cabin reeking of vomit and stink from the toilets, which were now in an unimaginable condition and had made the back portion of the aircraft worse than an animal stable. For most of the forty hours that the passengers had now spent inside the plane, there was little water to flush the sewage-clogged commodes. By the morning of 26 December, excreta was floating in the toilets, which were blocked and over-flowing with urine — and all this when passengers were avoiding having food and water to stay away from toilets. The urine had seeped into the passenger area, with shreds of used toilet paper floating on it. When nothing worked, some passengers laid out newspapers which they thought would absorb the urine. The newspapers were soon sub-merged. Then curtains were ripped off and laid on the aircraft floor. The stench was unbearable inside the aircraft, and many passengers vomited several times a day.

Outside, the jet was encircled on the tarmac by about two hundred Taliban soldiers with automatic weapons mounted on several vehicles, mainly Toyota pickup trucks. Diplomats from the Belgian, Spanish, Italian and Swiss embassies in Pakistan reached to help their nationals aboard the aircraft. In the airport building, dozens of jour-nalists were beginning to assemble after driving for hours across rugged terrain. Outside the Kandahar airport, more than twenty Taliban militiamen with rifles stood guard.

For Chief, it was time to get to work. UN official Erick du Mul landed in a white UN plane, met with the Taliban officials and was soon in the control tower, ready to start discussions with the hijackers. Discussions would go on with intervals throughout the day, and Athar was determined to be firm. He had already laid his cards on the table; now he suggested how the barter could be made. "We will release ten Indians and five foreigners from our side for each man released from Indian jails," he said in faltering English. Du Mul was negotiating from an extremely difficult position. He could not promise the hijackers anything on behalf of the Indian government, and yet he would have to hold out long enough to either let the Indians arrive and take over the negotiations, or for the hijackers to wear out. It was not clear what kind of role the UN had in the crisis — or whether it had a role at all. If India suggested that the UN had stepped in to help resolve the crisis, it could be extrapolated by the government's political rivals in New Delhi and armed rivals in Kashmir's battleground as the "internationalisation" of the Kashmir issue itself — a word Indian diplomats often try to ward off. The government's own contradiction would become clear when the prime minister said a day later: "India has not approached them. They must have come there on their own." Within hours, his Foreign Minister Jaswant Singh was saying just the opposite: "Mr. Erick du Mul has gone to Kandahar at our request to find out at first hand the conditions prevailing there."

The hijackers were revelling in the international attention their action was getting, but there was little that du Mul could do in the situation — and it was just a matter of time before Chief, or Ibrahim Athar, understood this compulsion.

And he did, in a few hours. Du Mul, who was to say later that the hijackers were "firm" and "determined," tried to find out who they were. He urged them to release the women and children. Chief was adamant and restive, often snapping and sounding irritated at the questions. For two hours they spoke by radio, their conversations peppered with long pauses and Chief's monologues about the situation in Kashmir and what he called oppression of innocent people by Indian forces. Outside the cockpit, Doctor was giving a similar speech on the public address system.

The aircraft's engines had been left running because of a malfunction — once shut down, the engines would not start again and the Taliban did not have the equipment needed to correct the problem. On the advice of the flight engineer, the hijackers also asked the Taliban to send jet engine oil, which would be needed to lubricate the engines of the A300. Then Jaggia himself stepped into the cockpit and spoke to du Mul: "The aircraft is in bad condition. It needs help. If possible, could you get Airbus Industrie people please?" The Taliban, in turn, called an engineer and a technician from its state-run Ariana Afghan Airlines, but they were not able to repair the plane for refuelling. Jaggia, who had earlier tried to buy time at the Al Minhad airport, kept telling Chief that the aircraft was not airworthy.

During one break in the negotiations, a Taliban official spoke on the radio set with Chief about Ripan Katyal's widow, Rachna. Ripan Katyal's widowed bride was asking too many questions, so she was sedated, and slept peacefully in her seat, still unaware her husband had been brutally killed, and was going to be cremated in New Delhi. She would be sedated at least four times during the rest of her imprisonment inside the plane, the injections coming each time she started looking desperately for her missing husband among the passengers. Katyal's parents and the Indian government had appealed to the hijackers to release her so that she could attend the funeral, and the Taliban official passed on the requests in the presence of reporters. The response was quick and firm. *"Hum yahan ek ya do logon ko chhorne nahin aaye hain"* (We haven't come here to release one or two people), Chief said. *"Hum yeh masla* India *ki* government *se poori tarah hal karna chahte hain"* (We want to resolve the issue with the Indian government thoroughly).

With those words, Ibrahim Athar had driven a second nail into the heart of a man far away in a cremation ground in New Delhi, one who was wailing loudly in crumpled clothes, dishevelled hair and a white stubble. Three weeks after the ecstasy of seeing his son bring home his daughter-in-law after their wedding, Chandra Mohan Katyal's young son lay in front of him, his lifeless body wrapped in a light blue blanket and embedded under a mound of white, red and yellow flowers, his eyes closed, his lips apart as if smiling a wry smile. The young woman his son had wedded was still hundreds of miles away, unable to see her husband one last time — completely unaware that he was dead. Ripan's father felt the chill of the winter afternoon, and stretched out his hand to cover his son's body in another blanket.

"Ripan mujhe bula raha hai ... voh so raha hai. Tu kyon so raha hai, Ripan? Apna chashma pehen le" (Ripan is calling me ... he is sleeping. Why are you sleeping, Ripan? Wear your spectacles), his father cried. *"Aankhe khol Babu! Aankhe khol, Babu"* (Open your eyes, Babu!), he screamed, crying like a child. Numbed by shock, the mother was not crying at all. Other weeping relatives held him and took him away. The family had preserved the body until 26 December, hoping that the hijackers would release his widow from the aircraft. After Chief rejected the request, the funeral was held, watched by hundreds of relatives, friends, and journalists. His parents ran to grab their son one more time as he was

being taken to be placed on the funeral pyre, but were pulled away once again.

In Kandahar, fear had melted a little for the hostage passengers. They were talking in hushed tones by now, though loud talking and laughing was not allowed — Chief had forbidden it. All the passengers became absolutely quiet when Chief stepped out of the cockpit, though he did so barely once a day. Those in the back rows were happy they were sitting there when Chief was outside the cockpit, because they always feared he could pick up one of them to be killed. Dr. Lalit Verma, an anaesthetist from the same Gurgaon town to which Ripan Katyal belonged, struck up a conversation with Shankar, the man of few words. In a rare moment when he indulged in a conversation more than just a few syllables, Shankar said he belonged to a militant group called Al Tehrik, to which Burger also belonged, and he and Doctor also had their brothers lodged in Indian jails for the last several years. The imprisonment of their kin seemed to be one of the key factors uniting the hijackers. Shankar claimed that Al Tehrik would organise more hijackings soon to get their relatives and colleagues released.

Several rows away, Burger was having a little fun with the children. He always seemed to have sweets, chocolates and smiles for the kids. He also had a few lessons for them. Burger put his gun into the hand of Himanshu Sharma, twelve, and asked him to hold it. *"Yeh* revolver *hai. Isme chheh goliyan hain"* (This is a revolver. It has six bullets), he told Himanshu, who was travelling with his family. Then he told the boy how to hold it, so Himanshu held it in his hand.

"*Dar lag raha hai?*" (Are you feeling scared?), Burger asked. "*Nahin*" (No), Himanshu said.

"*Agar koi cheez mangne se nahin milti hai to use bandook ki taqat se chheenna parta hai*" (If you don't get something by asking you have to snatch it with the power of the gun), Burger added.

Convinced that he would not survive the hijacking in the face of such fanaticism, passenger Sanjive Sharma was writing a last note for his wife Shiba, daughter Rukmini, son Shiv and other family members. On the back of a tattered red business class boarding card, the note read:

Har Shree Nath

Dear Shiba
  Give our children both me and you. Best of us. Ruku is brave. Give Shiv courage. Love you. You've been a lovely wife and mother.

Dear Brothers
  Give Shiba my share and I hope you guys can be brave. Miss you. Make Shiv and Ruku equal share in our property. God Bless.

Dear Mom and Dad,
  You have been the greatest parents I could ever have. May God make me your child in my next birth.

To: M.I.C/H.C./All Relatives
God Bless

To Neelu:
  Sorry I couldn't save Tukku

Love
Chitu

Neelu was the wife of his diabetic cousin Anil Khurana (Tukku), who sat next to him — and he was in a life threatening situation. After a long session at the radio set, Chief agreed in the afternoon to release Khurana, who was by then vomiting blood inside the plane and suffering from convulsions, Khurana was then rushed to the hospital again. Towards the evening, UN officials offered to airlift him to a hospital in Islamabad in a plane that was returning that evening to the Pakistani capital. Khurana, who refused to talk to reporters, insisted he would not leave until his cousin Sanjive Sharma and the other passengers were released as well. But he was later rushed to the Shifa Hospital in Islamabad as his condition worsened. Doctors diagnosed that his blood sugar level had shot up to 1,300 units.

Dr. Anita Joshi, who had attended to Khurana the previous evening, was herself in a precarious condition today, suffering from what she would describe later as a nervous breakdown. When the hijackers started their daily drill of threatening the passengers, forcing them to wear blindfolds again and declaring they would kill those who disobeyed, Dr. Joshi sprung from her seat and shouted at Burger: *"Chalo, mujhe mar do. Tum kisi se shuruat karna chahte ho na, to mujhe mar kar shuruat karo."* (Kill me. You want someone to start with, so start with me).

Others tried to figure out their own ways to cope with the crisis. Sanjive Sharma thought it might work if the passengers warmed up to the hijackers and pretended to empathise with them. He requested Burger to provide him a public address system, saying that he wanted to make a short speech to the passengers.

"Yeh achche log hain" (These are good people), he said of the hijackers. *"Yeh kaam yeh log zabardasti kar rahe hain kyonki hamari sarkar ne inke bhai-behnon ke saath badsalooki ki hai"*

(They are being forced to do this because our government has done injustice to their brothers and sisters).

Taliban officials began to pressure India into giving up its stance not to negotiate with the hijackers. Foreign Minister Wakil Ahmed Muttawakil said there was no immediate end to the crisis in sight, as the UN officials had failed in their negotiations. Having asserted a day before that the hijackers did not want to leave Afghanistan at any cost despite the Taliban's insistence, Muttawakil said the opposite on Sunday — that it could leave any time. He slammed India for not sending negotiators to broker an agreement with the hijackers. "India doesn't seem interested in what happens, in the passengers or in the plane," he told reporters. "They should send negotiators." Muttawakil also claimed that the aircraft had already been refuelled. As the flight engineer would say later, this was not true. His own colleague, Aviation Minister Akhtar Manzoor, said the Taliban regime was "ready to refuel the aircraft" and let the hijackers leave.

In New Delhi, with statements like these and little information on the fate of their kin, the suffering of the relatives was no less — actually much more — than that of the hostages. Television networks were beaming pictures of the beseiged plane standing in isolation in an alien country, with analyst after analyst trying to guess what would be happening inside. The experts painted frightening pictures of people wrecked by nervous breakdowns, heart attacks and brain haemorrhages — in turn, nearly bringing many among the helpless relatives to the verge of all these ailments. There was an information explosion around them, as television networks and newspapers strained to bring the hijacking, the hijacked plane and the hijackers themselves to the bedrooms of millions of viewers across the country. There was a flood of information on television on how the hijackers would be in the situation — edgy, furious, ready to kill; and how the hostages would be spending days in complete darkness with blindfolds on them all the time. But there was mostly no word from the government's side. There was also misinformation — officials started telling journalists that there were at least six hijackers on the plane: four Pakistanis, one Nepali and one Afghan. Gajendra Man Tamarkar, the Nepali businessman and part-time television comedian who was among the passengers, was described as the Nepali hijacker. Television networks lapped up the story and the villified Tamarkar quickly became a household name. It was only one of the several instances of bad reporting among the fiercely competitive networks — at one point midway through the crisis, one Indian network suddenly reported at the end of a bulletin, quoting CNN, that all the hostages had been released. In an attempt to keep pace with that "breaking story," a rival Indian network also reported the purported release of the passengers. The mystery was that CNN did not have any such story, and the reporters at the two networks had not bothered to confirm the story with Mohammad Khyber, the ATC official in Kandahar who had otherwise become a familiar feature on Indian news bulletins for his phone-in interviews.

Even days later, when it would be officially acknowledged that Tamarkar was not among the hijackers, no one would care to apologise.

The government was hopelessly short of information — so much so that once, when a senior aide of the prime minister walked out of his 7, Race Course residence where dozens of journalists were waiting for a briefing, he took a correspondent of an international news organisation aside. "Aaah, what's the latest? You know, you people are the only sources of information for us these days," he said, naming the reporter's organisation.

With little empathy from the government, the relatives decided to take things in their own hands. On 26 December, Foreign Minister Jaswant Singh had just started his daily afternoon press briefing in the conference hall of the Press Information Bureau when an unfamiliar crowd started assembling in the dimly lit corridor outside the hall. Singh, who was flanked by top officials of the external affairs ministry, answered the first question of the day as the relatives started to stream into the hall in a single file, and went and stood at some distance to the right of the minister. One man spoke out — this was Dr. Sanjeev Chhibber, six of whose relatives were on the aircraft. He introduced himself, and said how the government had not cared to explain to them what exacly was going on in Kandahar, or what they had planned to do to try to save the lives of their kin. He referred to a 1989 swap of terrorists to free a hostage, Rubaiya Sayeed, daughter of the then Home Minister Mufti Mohammad Sayeed. "If five terrorists can be freed to save the life of a minister's daughter, why not apply the same principle for our relatives? Are they not citizens of India?" Then the relatives began to shout their questions, and a lady among them broke down. Unflustered, Jaswant Singh heard them in silence and promised to explain to the relatives the compulsions of the government. When a journalist asked Singh whether the same principle could be applied in the hostage crisis as the Rubaiya Sayeed case, Singh brusquely snapped: "You are exploiting their concern." The relatives walked out of the hall, met separately with the minister, and then drove to the prime minister's residence to demonstrate outside the white metalled gates. It was the beginning of a string of noisy protests that partially forced the hand of the government on the crisis.

The change in stance became clear within hours, as the government assessed that the odds stacked against it were too many — the Taliban was showing an ambivalent stand, behaving itself and yet threatening to refuel the aircraft, the hijackers were showing no signs of climbing down from their demands, and the clamour of the anguished relatives was echoing across the country, shaping popular opinion. From the high and tough moral stand taken by Prime Minister Vajpayee a day ago when he said India would not bow to terrorism, the government stood a notch lower in that battle against the hijackers on Sunday. Foreign Minister Jaswant Singh said India was "examining" the hijackers' demands, and would "exercise every option" for the hostages' release. Singh did not say yes or no when asked whether Maulana Masood Azhar could be released. "It's not a yes-and-no answer to which I can address myself," Singh told reporters. "I will exercise all options towards the aim of ensuring the well-being of passengers." Seeking political backing for any decision, Vajpayee called a meeting of opposition parties at his residence in the evening, before meeting the full Cabinet for the first time after the crisis broke out.

But before that, it was time for another gaffe. At the end of his daily press briefing, just before he got up to leave, Jaswant Singh dropped a bombshell in the room full of journalists. In response to a question, he casually said that the hijackers — now the minister was calling them "five hijackers" — reached Kathmandu on a Pakistan International Airlines plane, waited in the transit lounge, were handed tickets by an accomplice and then just walked to the departure lounge to board the aircraft. The room suddenly seemed to erupt. Journalists of rival news organisations rushed out loudly dictating the story to their colleagues in their offices on their mobile phones. As Singh rose from his seat, a reporter walked up to Singh and asked him where he thought the flight had originated.

"The flight was coming from ... Actually I'd rather not say all this," Singh said, smiled, and walked off. The truth was Singh did not know, and had made an unusually prominent blunder. His statement was apparently based on a version from some officials which, in turn, seemed curiously similar to an unsubtantiated story on a domestic television network. The statement was slammed by the Pakistan International Airlines, the Nepal government, and surprisingly by the state-owned Indian Airlines as well. There was a gap of at least five hours between the PIA flight and the Indian Airlines flight. And there is no transit lounge at the Tribhuvan International Airport.

Across the border and at about the same time, Pakistan's Foreign Minister Abdul Sattar made another statement that also sounded like balderdash: he claimed that the Research and Analysis Wing, India's external intelligence agency, had plotted the hijacking to malign Pakistan's new military rulers. "The possibility can no longer be ignored that the incident involves a preconceived design by a foreign intelligence organisation," Sattar said straight-faced at a press conference in Islamabad, a day after the main hijacker had already identified himself as the brother of the Pakistani cleric Azhar. "Perhaps the government of India manufactured another incident in pursuit of their aim of maligning Pakistan internationally," he alleged.

Away from the diplomatic wars, the hostages and the hostage-takers had their most loved ones on their minds.

A young woman from New Delhi who was on vacation with her husband had a much more important task to finish inside the aircraft. The woman, who would later ask not to be named, was writing a farewell letter to her four-year-old daughter, having given up on the belief that she would ever meet her. She scribbled on the back of a Christmas card from the hotel in which she had stayed in Kathmandu:

"I have not always been the best of mothers, but please always know that I loved you very much. Please be strong and God will take care of you. You are not old enough to read this right now but one day I hope you will."

She then wanted to give it to the persons who she thought had the best chance to survive the hijacking — the hijackers themselves. She requested them to keep the letter and find a way to have it sent to her daughter, but none of the men wanted to take the letter.

While the young woman waited to get another opportunity to hand over the letter to the hijackers, a group of traders in seats nearby was discussing something that was close to their hearts — the prices of paints.

Further down the aisle, Sanjive Sharma was deep in thought and tears welled up in his eyes thinking about his young son Shiv, and a little chat they had had the night before Sharma took the flight to Kathmandu with his cousin Anil Khurana, the diabetes patient. For no reason, Shiv embraced him very tightly, started crying, and asked his father to give him a warm hug. Before Sharma could understand what was on his son's mind, Shiv said, still in tears: *"Papa, agar tum mar gaye na, to main tumko vahin aa kar bahut maroonga"* (Papa, if you die, I'll come there and thrash you).

Sharma was stunned to hear his son talk about death.

"Main kyon maroonga, Shiv? *Main nahin maroonga"* (Why should I die, Shiv? I won't die), he said.

"Promise?"

"Promise."

Sharma broke down and started crying himself as he related this story to Burger. *"Main apne bete ko* ditch *nahin karna chahta"* (I dont want to ditch my son), he said.

"Insha'Allah, tum apna promise *rakhoge"* (Allah willing, you'll keep your promise), Burger replied. *"Meri do mahine ki beti hai aur maine use ab tak dekha nahin hai."* (I have a two-month-old daughter and I haven't seen her so far).

Afghani rotis, called khatoos, and rajma was served for dinner at 9:30 p.m., and, as if it was something that was mixed in the food, the hijackers immediately transformed into their ruthless versions.

Burger soon shed the sentimental mask. He screamed at a man who was crying, and announced he would kill the passenger who sought favours from him or cried. *"Mere bhai jail mein hain. Unko torture karte hain. Tum mar jaoge to tumhari bodies tumhare rishtedar le jaenge"* (My brothers are in jail. They are tortured. If you die, your relatives will collect your bodies), he bellowed.

Rajeev Ahuja, the eighth man to be tied up when Katyal was killed — and the man who earned the severest rebukes from the hijackers — was about to have another of those bouts of ill luck. His blindfold, which had slipped off on the first night and got him nearly killed, slipped off again. He looked around. It was all quiet in the plane.

Everybody appeared to be sleeping.

Except one. Doctor, who was keeping watch from a corner, came running down the aisle, and hit Ahuja hard on his face. Ahuja cried out in pain and tears came to his eyes. He wanted to see if he was bleeding, but was too terrified to move even his finger while Doctor was there. As Doctor stood staring at him, he finally mustered the courage to utter four words, *"Aapne mujhe kyon mara?"* (Why did you hit me?) Doctor was furious. He ignored the question, and said; *"Meri baat sun le. Kal subah tujhe aage le kar jaenge aur tera kaam kar denge"* (Take my word; Tomorrow morning you're dead). Ahuja trembled with fear all night and got ready to die at the hands of the man who had already claimed one life.

But before morning came, there were two surprises.

At about 11 p.m., the hijackers started their familiar nightly drill — they ordered the blindfolds again. They were in a hurry. Passengers were slapped for not closing their eyes, they were shouted at, and the four men in the passenger cabin suddenly became the monsters that the passengers had forgotten for a few hours. As if there was something the hijackers wanted to do away from the prying eyes of the passengers, every one was ordered to go to sleep. Burger ran down the aisle, back and forth, several times. Shankar removed the pin from his hand grenade. Bhola kept watch in the front portion, ready with a revolver. There was total silence among the passengers. After a while, the hijackers stopped shouting as well. They seemed edgy and tense.

Suddenly, there was a volley of gunfire that several passengers heard coming from outside the plane. It seemed like a gun salute, followed by slogans that the Taliban soldiers were roaring with gusto. After some minutes, passengers sitting near the front exit heard the door open. There was shuffling of feet. Someone had walked into the plane. It was someone very important — the hijackers did not say anything apart from muttering a slow Islamic religious chant. No one dared raise their heads. Several minutes passed. The visitor seemed to look around, and then he walked out. The door closed.

Days later, the hostages were told of the crucial role that Mullah Omar had played in the hostages crisis. Those who had heard a man come in on the night of 26 December after being given gun salutes wondered: was the visitor Mullah Omar?

After about an hour, Burger broke the ice. "*Sar utha sakte hain*" (You can raise your heads now), he ordered. As puzzled passengers looked up, he surprised them further and said: "*Kuchh bolo bhi. Koi chutkula sunao*" (Say something, crack a joke). Some people actually mustered their nerves and thought up a few jokes. It was nearly midnight. Others were still waiting expectantly for their release promised at nine by Burger. They gave up hope after a while and started drifting off to sleep.

The second surprise came an hour or so later, and it was, for the time being, only for one man: Flight Engineer Anil Jaggia. He was dozing.

Shankar walked up to Flight Engineer Jaggia's seat, woke him up and put a gun to his head. The hijackers wanted Jaggia to come down with them and open the baggage hold. A step ladder had already been arranged with help from the Taliban. It was wheeled up to the aircraft in the dark. Holding a large red torch, Jaggia went down through the metal ladder that was lowered from inside the cockpit. There were headlights all around him. Several Taliban soldiers watched from their vehicles and from the tarmac as Shankar and Burger stood next to him, holding guns to his head. "Open it. *Humne* ATC *se permission le li hai*" (We have permission from the ATC), Burger said.

Jaggia, the most senior crew member by age, tried to avert this the best he could. He whiled away time, pretending he could not open the baggage hold. The hijackers were getting impatient. Jaggia insisted on speaking with the ATC. No one was available in the control tower. "We need something urgently," Burger said. Finally, the hold was opened and Shankar climbed up the step ladder. He rummaged inside for a while, and finally took out a large bag. The contents — an assortment of sophisticated weapons — were taken up to the cockpit. Jaggia returned to his seat.

As there were only Bhola and Doctor guarding the whole plane now, with Chief sleeping in the business class, French passenger Francoise Jougla, forty-five, and other passengers managed to peep from between seats and saw the hijackers haul up olive green crates, and then watched in horror as they reloaded their revolvers.

When everything was inside, the contents of the crates and the bag were emptied inside the cockpit. It was like an arms bazaar — there was a frightening display of machine guns, pistols, grenades and ammunition, strewn carelessly all over the cockpit. There were several AK47 and AK56 machine guns; grenades were piled up like an assortment of firecrackers and kept on the raised tables and the observer's seat behind that of the pilot. There were dozens of Israeli-made 9 mm Uzi sub-machine-guns, fully automatic and one of the most sophisticated in their class, used for close-quarter battle; and an array of automatic pistols.

Bullets, which had been brought packed in dozens of small cardboard boxes as small as cigarette packets, were thrown carelessly on a table behind the co-pilot's seat.

Some of it was part of what Shankar took out from the luggage hold. For the rest of the weapons, there was only one place it could have come from: the Taliban.

DAY

4

---

*Several passengers' lives are saved in the nick of time
as India agrees to send its negotiators to Kandahar,
as relatives beg the government to take action to free
the hostages ... but Chief is adamant on
Masood Azhar's release.*

Cycle-rickshaws fought for space with noisy scooters,
fume-spewing cars and wooden luggage trolleys on the
narrow road in Kanpur city. It was a sunny Monday and
a group of young boys had gathered in a small grocer's
shop in the predominantly Muslim neighbourhood. As they
would tell the police later, they had come to hear what they
were told was an exciting taped speech. In minutes, a man
appeared with a cassette player, and the boys craned their
necks to hear above the din of the traffic outside. The man
speaking was Maulana Masood Azhar, in an address years
ago at a religious school in Pakistan where he had gone to
recruit fighters. It was one of those tapes that had circulated

in thousands across the Muslim world. Abdul Latif, the main accomplice of Chief, had bought one of them in Jeddah.

"*Nahin chahiye mujhe voh naujawan jo Islam ki qeemat par* hockey *aur* cricket *ke qayal hain. Mujhe chahiye jawan josheelay mard jo duniya bhar mein Islam ki rehnumaee karenge aur qafiron ke khilaf jehad karenge A K saintalees,* rocket launcher *aur* pistol *ki taaqat par,"* Azhar bellowed in his speech, interspersed with cheers and religious slogans. (I am not interested in the youth who are inclined towards hockey or cricket at the cost of Islam. I need young and energetic men, committed to the revival of Islam around the world with AK47s, pistols, rocket launchers for a successful jehad against non-believers). As the speech ended, a man's voice echoed in the background: "*Allahumma Labbaik, Al jehad.*" Gunshots were fired in the air.

The cassette has been in circulation for years, but it had surfaced again in several states across India, from Himachal Pradesh to Assam, after the hijacking drama began, and after it became known that the release of Masood Azhar was the main goal of the hostage-takers. The tape had the potential to fan religious riots, and as word spread about it, the police seized several copies within hours.

It was the fourth day of the hostage crisis. The hijacking had gripped the nation, and it had overtaken the two top stories until a few days ago: the Y2K bug and the millennium. In thousands of homes, the television became the only window to the gruelling, gut-wrenching crisis. People who never had anything to do with listening to the news waited for fresh updates. In letters to editors, in phone-in programmes and in drawing room conversations, people were getting desperate. They wanted the plane to be stormed. They wanted the hijackers to be given the worst possible punishment. Grandmothers and mothers grieved and empathised with Rachna Katyal, the woman who was widowed in three weeks. In street-corner gossip and coffee table talk, people suggested to each other how the hijackers should be killed. Furious young men called television networks to suggest that the militants whose release was demanded by the hijackers should be executed in public. Others wanted them to be released, but only after being infected with the AIDS virus, or a medicine which would automatically kill them some hours after the hostages were free. Some wanted miniature time bombs to be planted inside the bodies of the militants before freeing them. By default, the hijackers had given a common voice of anger and anguish to a billion Indians.

And one word was being mentioned again and again: Entebbe.

The hijacking was beginning to seem like a replay of a 1976 hijacking of an Air France aircraft — also an Airbus 300 — on 27 June 1976. Four armed men, two Palestinians and two Germans, hijacked Flight 139 flying from Israel's Ben Gurion Airport to France, boarding the plane at a stop-over at Athens, taking advantage of lax security. After a stopover at Lybia's Benghazi Airport for refuelling, the plane was forced to land at Entebbe in Uganda, then governed by dictator Idi Amin, a former friend of Israel who had now turned against it. One hundred and four Israelis and Jews were selected to be kept as hostages.

Like Flight 814, the Air France flight had been hijacked to free a jailed religious leader and other pro-Palestinian prisoners — fifty-three in all, in Israel, Kenya and Europe. Maulana Masood Azhar seemed a Pakistani version of the religious guru that the terrorists at Entebbe had wanted to free: Bishop Hilarion Capucci, being kept in an Israeli prison cell in Ramla, a tall, arrogant preacher with a long flowing beard, saluted even by prison guards. Like Azhar, Capucci was treated like a special prisoner. Also, like Azhar would twenty years later, Capucci had told his captors after his arrest in 1974 that they would not be able to keep him behind bars for long.

The Air France plane was in a country which was expected only to help the hijackers. So the Israeli government defied the Ugandan government and flew four planeloads of commandos to Entebbe to execute Operation Thunderball on 3 July. In fifty-three minutes, the operation was over. Two hostages were killed and ten wounded, of whom one later died in hospital.

The question was haunting India's government: Would Kandahar be an Entebbe?

In Kandahar, the passengers had woken up and were astonished to see there were more arms with the hijackers now. Despite that, it seemed a promising day — the hijackers allowed the passengers to slide up their shutters, for the first time. The sight that the passengers saw outside was spine-chilling: there were gun-toting men in turbans, vehicles with Stinger missiles and rocket launchers, below the plane, on the tarmac. For the first time, the passengers realised where they were.

Monday was passenger Pooja Kataria's birthday. As passengers woke up and word spread about her birthday, Burger walked up to her and took off a shawl he was wearing. Then he wrote on it with a pen: "To our dear sister Pooja, with lots of love and wishes." She would say later: "They were not all that cruel people."

But Monday was also the day when Doctor had promised to kill Rajeev Ahuja. Soon he found a reason as well.

Taliban militiamen in pickup trucks arrive at the hijacked Indian Airlines plane to beef up security in Kandahar, as Indian negotiators haggle with the hijackers on how many Kashmiri militants should be released.

The staff of Kandahar airport fill bottles with water from a tap for the hijacked passengers of IC 814.

Taliban soldiers, armed with U.S.-made heat-seeking surface-to-air stinger missiles, drive past the hijacked plane.

Ibrahim Athar @ Chief

Sunny Ahmed Qazi
@ Burger @ Mansoor

Shahid Akhtar Sayeed
@ Doctor @ Khalid

Mugshots of hijackers

Rajesh Gopal Verma @ Shakir

Mistri Zahur Ibrahim @ Bhola

Relatives of hijacked passengers weep outside the venue of a briefing for them in New Delhi, as the hijackers threatened to begin killing passengers if their demands were not met.

A passenger's relative weeps outside the Prime Minister's House in New Delhi.

A grim relative reacts during an official briefing in New Delhi.

Relatives of passengers block traffic outside the Prime Minister's House, in protest against the Indian government's dragging its feet in helping resolve the hostage situation.

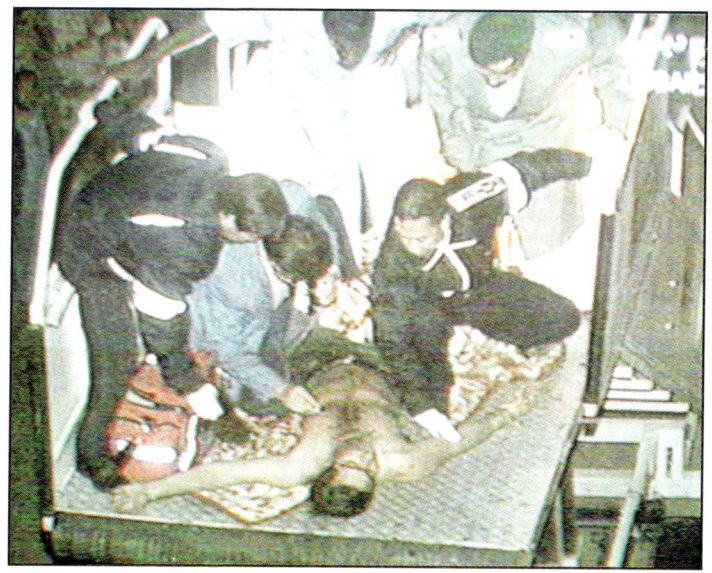

*Medical workers at Dubai airport examine the body of Ripan Katyal,
a passenger who was killed by the hijackers even as his wife,
Rachna, also on the plane, was kept in the dark about it. The
hijackers released the body, along with 26 passengers, in Dubai
before taking off for Kandahar.*

A file photo of Ripan Katyal and his wife Rachna in happier times.

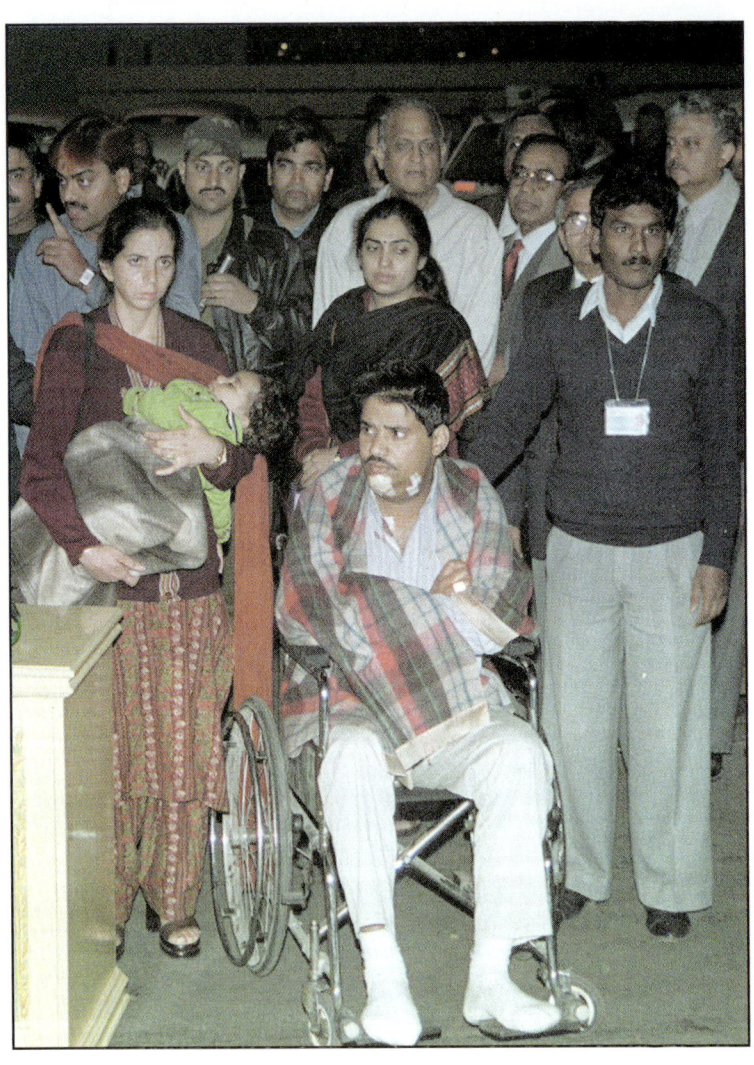

Passengers released in Dubai arrive at New Delhi. In wheelchair is Satnam Singh, who was stabbed by the hijackers.

Members of the Indian negotiating team relax in the sun at Kandahar airport, as the impasse between them and the hijackers continues.

A masked hijacker ('Doctor') in checked trousers, and a Taliban official and an Indian Airlines engineer look at the hijacked aircraft after repair work. The plane's engines had shut down, interrupting talks and cutting radio communications.

One of the five hijackers ('Burger') descends from the cockpit holding a pistol at Kandahar airport, minutes before they and the released militants drove away in waiting vehicles.

Hijacker Bhola searches a Taliban hostage (brother of the Kandahar corps commander) for guns just before the eight-day-long drama came to an end.

Hijackers 'Doctor' and 'Shankar' escort a Taliban hostage to a waiting car.

One week after their aircraft was hijacked, the passengers are taken by bus to a waiting aircraft which will fly them back to India.

The hijacking over, the empty Indian Airlines plane takes off from Kandahar for New Delhi. The passengers left earlier by another flight

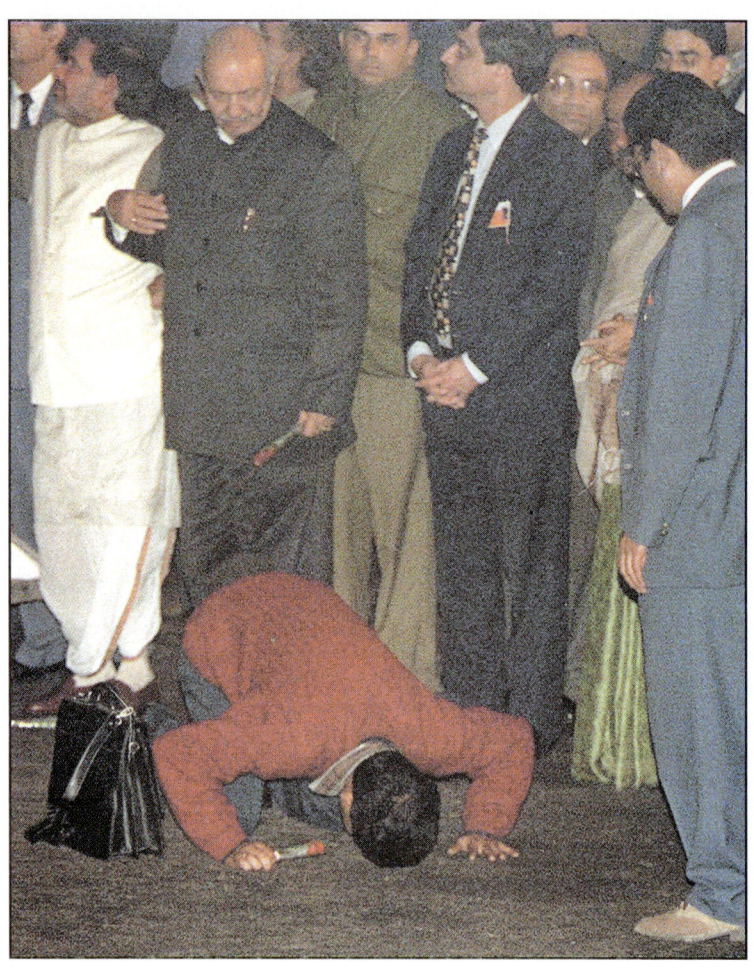

A hostage kisses the ground after disembarking from a plane at Indira Gandhi International Airport in New Delhi.

Rachna, the widow of Ripan Katyal, is helped from the plane at Indira Gandhi International Airport.

D. Sharan, captain of the hijacked plane, gets a hero's welcome as he arrives in New Delhi from Kandahar.

*Prime Minister Vajpayee greets freed hostage Anil Khurana, a
diabetic who was released in Kandahar, and his wife in New Delhi.*

Surrounded by armed guards, released cleric Maulana Masood Azhar (seated) roams unhindered and addresses supporters at his hometown in Bahawalpur, Pakistan, on Eid ul-Fitr.

Maulana Masood Azhar arrives at Karachi airport. Like Azhar, the five hijackers too are believed to have found shelter in Pakistan.

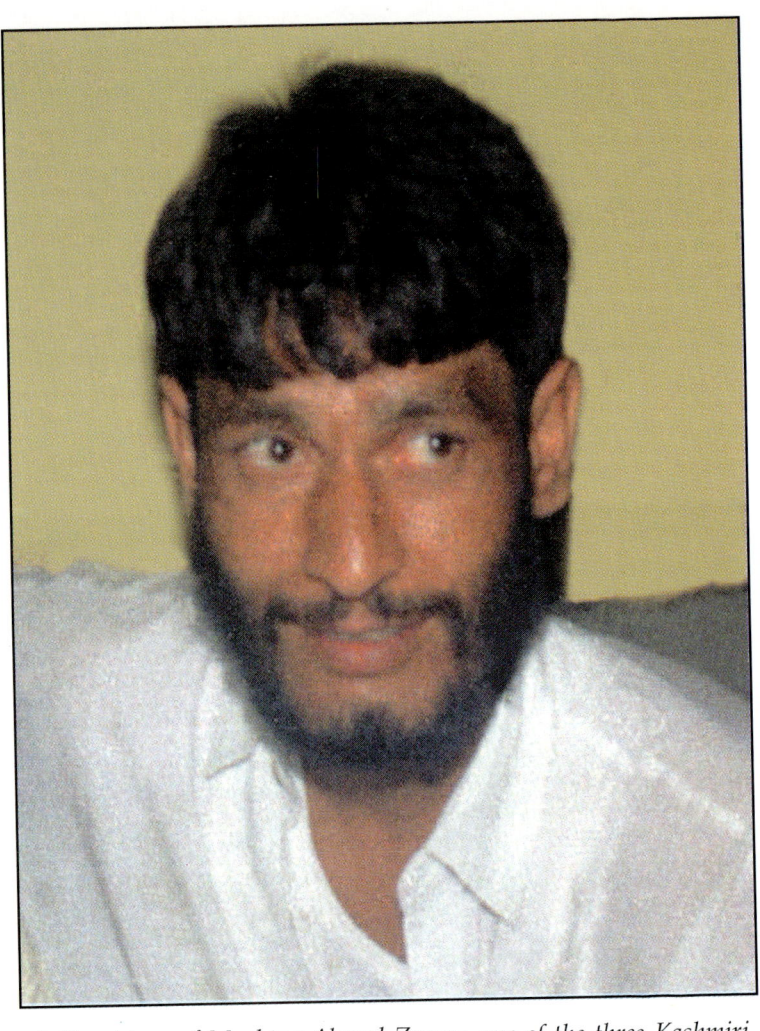

A file picture of Mushtaq Ahmed Zargar, one of the three Kashmiri militants released in exchange for hostages. Zargar is believed to be in Pakistan-occupied Kashmir.

Chief was inside the cockpit, talking since morning with Erick du Mul. It was getting nowhere. They seemed to be repeating the same things and the same arguments again and again — du Mul requesting them to free the women and children, Chief declaring he would now not settle for any truncated deal and wanted a final settlement of the "dispute." They were running around in circles. There was no sign of Indian negotiators, and the hijackers were beginning to believe they were being taken for granted by the Indian authorities. They were not being taken seriously enough. So Chief needed to send a signal to the Indians that they meant business — they needed to kill a few hostages. At about 9:30 a.m., Chief flared up. He started shouting threats on the radio. He wanted his demands to be fulfilled immediately.

"We are giving you ten minutes! We are giving you ten minutes!" he shouted. Meanwhile, Doctor, who was standing by, grew furious.

He took Bhola with him, both holding their weapons, and walked towards the economy class taking long strides. Doctor pointed towards Rajeev Ahuja and angrily shouted at the air hostesses: "*Munh par kapda lagao!*" (Blindfold him!) Ahuja, who sat terrified in his seat, barely looking up as he heard the two hijackers coming towards him, had not been able to sleep the whole night. A nervous air hostess quickly tied a blindfold on Ahuja's face. His hands were tied to the back. Doctor held Ahuja's collar in his tight grasp, and yanked him from his seat. Then he pushed him cruelly towards the business class. Ahuja had gotten away two nights ago, but today Doctor seemed determined to kill him.

"*Maine kya kiya hai? Maine kya kiya hai?* Please *mujhe chhor do*, please" (What have I done? Please spare me), he

[99]

cried. Unable to see anything, Ahuja pleaded like a frightened child, his words getting lost in a terrified whimper as he started weeping. Death seemed right there, so Ahuja wriggled, and tried to pull his hand away from Doctor's iron-tight grip as they stood in front of the business class seats. This made Doctor even more angry. He held Ahuja by the scruff of his collar and shook him up. It seemed like a scene from the dramatic climax of a Hindi film.

"Agar tu girgirana nahin band karega to hum tujhe marenge nahin, tere tukre kar denge. Bahut dard hoga." (If you don't stop begging like this, we will not just kill you, we will cut you into pieces. There'll be great pain).

"Tumhari sarkar ko tumhari koi fiqr nahin hai. Humne unse kaha hum derh sau log mar denge, vo bole mar do, hamein fikr nahin hai" (Your government does not give a damn about you. We told them we would kill 150 people; they said do it, we don't care). *"Jab tak hum dus barah ko kat kar runway par nahin phekenge, yeh samjhenge nahin"* (Until we kill 10-12 people and throw their bodies on the runway, the Indians will not understand).

Bhola held one of his arms and pulled Ahuja towards him. *"Iska I-card nikalo"* (Take out his identity card). Ahuja finally gave up. In a second, he imagined exactly what he thought was going to happen; he would be killed, his body would be thrown on the runway, and his name would be announced from his identity card, which would be thrown on his body.

Inside the cockpit, Chief had announced the most serious ultimatum since he had landed in Kandahar. He had promised du Mul that he would start killing passengers in ten minutes if the demands were not met — which is why Ahuja was brought to the business class to be killed. After being persuaded by the negotiator, he extended the deadline by three hours to 0830 GMT (1240 local time).

Ahuja heard the cockpit door open, and then Chief spoke out. *"Vo baat karne ko tayyar hain.* Indian government *ko teen ghante ka waqt diya hai. Ise abhi chhor do, jaane do"* (They are willing to talk. I have given the Indian government three hours' time. Let it be, let him go). He was untied and sent back to his seat. Then the same air hostess walked up to him again. "Sir? Will you have some water? Will you have something to eat?" she said. As Ahuja would describe later, he finally felt reassured that he would live.

But, suddenly, tension soared at the airport. There was a flurry of activity. Alarmed that the Taliban's inaction and possible bloodshed on its territory could only entrench its image as a patron of militant activity, Afghan officials ordered its soldiers to surround the jet.

In New Delhi, the cauldron of patience finally spilled over. For three days, the helpless relatives of the hostages had done things that none of them would ever have imagined themselves doing in their professional and personal lives — they had squatted on roads, begged officials for information, screamed at a press conference and fainted in each other's arms. Today, as news spread of the deadline set by the hijackers after which they would start killing passengers, it raised visions before the relatives of their kin being killed, as if before their own eyes as they watched helplessly. Dozens of people jostled and punched and pushed at a gathering at the Centaur Hotel where government officials were briefing them on the crisis. Men stood on chairs and screamed at the officials, demanding to know if the reports of the deadline were true. Several people started crying. The more aggressive abused the government. Some shook their fists and raised slogans. Others toppled chairs in shock and disbelief.

Finally, they begged.

"There is no time," one man said, his hands folded respectfully, tears in his eyes. "Please tell us where can we meet the senior officials. We go to the prime minister's house, they ask us to go to the Rajiv Gandhi Bhavan. Then you say you have no news. Where should we go?"

The civil aviation ministry official dialled a number on his cellular phone and told the relatives that the CMG was meeting at the Rajiv Gandhi Bhavan at the civil aviation ministry. The crowd took along H.S. Khola, director-general of civil aviation from the hotel. In minutes, a caravan of nearly thirty cars was speeding on the roads, driven by frenzied drivers zigzagging their way through the busy intersections, ignoring all traffic lights.

Security guards at the ministry building stopped them. The huge black iron gates were closed and locked. Dozens of men pleaded to be let in, then sat down helplessly by the road. Forty minutes passed. The deadline was near. Then, the crowd rose, like a wave, and swept past the huge iron gates, some climbing over the rails, others breaking open the locks. Waving batons and screaming orders, police officers stood stunned as they were jostled, heckled and brushed aside. Slogans against the government echoed in the air; so did expletives. One after the other, senior officials stepped out of their offices and tried to explain to them that the hostages were safe, that negotiators were being sent. Nothing worked. They wanted nothing short of the prime minister of India coming to assure them. The angry caravan drove off again, and reached the official residence of the prime minister. Several people lay down on the road not knowing how else to express their ultimate helplessness.

Some relatives said they would kill themselves. Others beat their chests. They looked at their watches, again and again. The crowd tried to storm past the ring of security guards at the 7, Race Course Road residence.

"We have voted him to power. Can't we even meet him now?" an old woman screamed as she pushed away a woman police constable trying to stop her from walking towards Vajpayee's residence.

Four women sitting continents apart knew exactly how the shattered, desperate crowd was feeling.

Thousands of kilometres to the west at her home in the US town of Orefield in Pennsylvania state, Jane Schelly was looking at her watch repeatedly as she sat watching the news on television. The hijacking was one of the top stories, and she was calculating the time in India as the deadline neared, feeling the sense of helplessness that the hostages' relatives were overcome by. Schelly was the wife of Donald Hutchins, the American tourist abducted along with five other foreigners in Kashmir on 4 July 1995, one of the early attempts to free Maulana Masood Azhar. The fate of her psychologist husband is still not known for certain, though he is believed to have been killed by the terrorists.

As she watched the story on television, she hoped the terrorists would be able to provide some information on her husband as well. For Schelly, the agony — of being separated from a loved one and not knowing what happened to him — has lasted nearly five years, and it still festers. She had knocked on the doors of President Bill Clinton, Secretary of State Madeleine Albright, the FBI, two Pakistani prime ministers, Indian officials and religious and militant leaders. When that did not work, she travelled to remote villages, mosques and bus stations in Pakistan to distribute flyers that include her husband's photograph. She has spent every summer since 1995 in Kashmir looking for her husband.

She also met Masood Azhar, for whose freedom her husband was taken captive, at the high security Tihar prison in New Delhi on 4 July 1996. Schelly, who remembered Azhar as articulate and intelligent, begged him for help. Speaking in English, Azhar asked her: "What can I do?" He agreed to issue an appeal on a humanitarian basis for the release of the captives.

Across the Atlantic Ocean in Britain, another woman had seen Masood Azhar's face on television, and it sent shivers down her spine. As Julie would say later in a newspaper interview: "I was shocked to see his face again on TV and hear his name." Julie Mangan was the wife of Keith Mangan, another of the six Western hostages abducted to free Azhar, and December 26, the day she first saw Azhar's face on television after years, would have been her husband's birthday.

In 1997, one year after Jane Schelly met Masood Azhar, Julie Mangan had also walked with hope to the prison cell of Azhar, who had by then been transferred to Jammu's Kot Bhalwal jail. She returned disappointed, and would remember him as a "cold, callous man." The hijack drama "brings back all the pain of how he could have helped us but never did," she said.

One of the six hostages fled, two were killed, and the fate of the rest remained unknown. It was a tragic coincidence that according to a jailed terrorist, they were also killed on Christmas Eve, 1995. The Indian Airlines plane was hijacked exactly four years later.

Two women were watching the hostage drama closely in Kashmir — and reliving their own days as hostages taken by Kashmiri militants. Rubaiya Sayeed, daughter of the then Union Home Minister Mufti Mohammad Sayeed and Naheed Soz, daughter of former Union Forest Minister Prof. Saifuddin Soz, were taken hostage in 1989 and 1991 respectively and released in exchange for militants. "I can never forget those eleven days in the captivity of the militants," Naheed Soz said in a newsaper interview. "Being a hostage is horrifying as every second passes with the fear of getting killed. The government should not waste time, the hijackers can do anything."

Naheed Soz was right. In Kandahar, the hijackers were now determined to do anything. Before they could carry out their threat of killing the passengers, they were denying them food. Angry at the delay in the arrival of the Indian delegation, the hijackers refused to take food for the passengers all of 27 December. The water left from the previous day had run out, and everyone scrounged for the remaining bottles.

The deadline for the killings was coming closer. There was no word about the Indian delegation arriving. Chief wanted to make sure this ultimatum to kill passengers was not shrugged off as a false alarm. He opened the cockpit door and asked for Burger. Having got his instructions, Burger ran down the aisle, concentrating on the seats on the left side where most foreign passengers were sitting, and stopped by one row. He asked two men — one a Spanish man, and the other a Belgian — to step out. They were taken to the business class, which had by now been designated in the minds of the passengers as something of an execution chamber. Burger commanded the men to sit down, and went through the drill of tying blindfolds on them and tying their hands at the back. A short while later, passengers in the front rows heard him scream: "I will shoot you if you open your eyes! If you move I will shoot you!"

Two more heads were ready for the execution block, and the hijackers knew India would have some explaining to do if harm came to them. Chief told the negotiator about the two hostages being tied up, and it was only when du Mul told them repeatedly that an Indian official was on the way, that they let the two men go back to their seats.

Du Mul also spoke to Capt. Sharan, whose role had become very limited after landing in Kandahar. The pilot sounded another warning: "The plane will crash — 100 per cent — if we take off from Afghanistan. I am very tired, I cannot fly the plane."

In the zero-sum game, India took the first step. A short while before the deadline was to expire, A.R. Ghanshyam, counsellor at the Indian High Commission in Islamabad, arrived in Kandahar. He immediately walked to the control tower and spoke with Chief on radio, setting up the first direct communication between the Indian government and the hijackers. After a brief and tense discussion, he reported back to New Delhi: the hijackers were holding on, and they seemed determined to start killing the passengers if a team of Indian negotiators did not arrive from New Delhi as soon as possible.

This time, India's response was swift. Foreign Minister Jaswant Singh announced in New Delhi that a 52-member team would leave for Kandahar immediately. This was conveyed instantly to Chief in the cockpit.

He suspended the deadline, and then stepped into the economy class for the first time that day. There was a sudden hush among the passengers. "*Ek achhi khabar hai.* Indian delegation *humse baatcheet ke liye aaj shaam ko aa raha hai*"

(There is some good news. The Indian delegation is arriving in the evening to talk to us).

The Taliban also extracted its price: Muttawakil asked for 25,000 US dollars in landing rights for the second plane bringing the negotiators. There was no choice but to pay.

For the next two hours, the hijackers lowered their guard. The passengers did not see them; they were either outside the plane or huddled in the cockpit brainstorming for the negotiations with the Indian team. The shades in the plane remained drawn and the engines were running. For the passengers, the arrival of the negotiators was the first piece of promising news that they had heard since the arrival of the UN official. Finally things seemed to be moving outside the hostage aircraft. But the conditions inside the aircraft were already much worse. Four seats had been soiled by blood and Katyal's blood-soaked clothes still lay on one side. All along the aisles, there were chicken bones, scraps of paper, beer cans, stains of vomit and fruit juice, paper napkins, cigarette butts, tobacco packets, broken pieces of bread and strewn grains of cooked rice. In the rear, carpets and rubber mats were damaged after being drenched in urine for two days. The stink was worse than that of a public lavatory. All newspapers and magazines on board had been used up — by the passengers as well as their captors — as toilet paper. Many people were beginning to rip off seat covers. There was a squelching noise as people walked on the carpets. When the stench became unbearable, the passengers took permission from the hijackers to rummage in their hand baggage for room fresheners that they had bought in Kathmandu. When that too ran out, they started using the perfume bottles and Eau de Cologne they had bought. But after every few hours, nothing seemed to be working. Passengers got to develop so much revulsion for going to the toilet, that some asked doctors on board for medicine to force constipation.

Luckily for the hostages, before the economy class started resembling a manhole, Taliban men walked into the aircraft to clean the toilets. There would be some reprieve. The hijackers frisked the cleaners and warned them not to speak with or look at the hostages. Surprisingly, they spoke in Pashtu, the language of the Afghans, the language that Ibrahim Athar was once overheard speaking inside the cockpit when he was on the radio set. Passenger Sanjive Sharma listened hard as the hijackers spoke to the cleaners — his mother is from Pakistan's Peshawar city and he had been to Afghanistan several times as a child while family elders went on tours for their dry fruit business. The hijackers' knowledge of Pashtu was not surprising, since most members of the Harkat-ul Mujahideen, to which India and the US say the hijackers belonged, undergo training at a military camp in Afghanistan's Khost region allegedly run by Pakistan's Inter Services Intelligence — the same camp where Maulana Masood Azhar said he was found unfit for training.

Large green tents were pitched inside the airport premises where doctors from the international federation of the Red Cross had stocked emergency supplies of medicines. There were basic medicines, mainly for muscular pain, headaches, nausea and stress. But at least one patient had also been put on intravenous fluid, and another, who could not take the physical strain of sitting with his head bowed, was rushed emergency supplies after he seemed to have temporarily gone into coma and his body began to turn blue. There were three Indian doctors and a French one among the hostages, and several times a day, they sent requests to the medical staff outside for supplies of medicines.

As the hostages waited for hours, the hijackers started slamming the Indian government for its alleged excesses in Kashmir, and for what they called washing their hands off the hostages.

"Kaisi hai ye tumhari sarkar? Tumhe to chullu bhar paani mein doob marna chahiye. Teen din ho gaye aur vo tumhare liye kuchch bhi nahin karna chahte" (What kind of a government is this? You should die in shame. Three days have passed, and they don't want to do anything for you).

Something unusual was happening in the Jammu prison. Prisoners had suddenly developed a keen interest in listening to the news.

From their prison barracks and cells, Maulana Masood Azhar's fellow inmates were passionately following the hijacking drama, glued to their radio transistor sets. Each evening, the barracks were submerged in noisy slogans in a raucous celebration of the hostage-taking. It became a security problem, and in a jail from where three prisoners had escaped in 1998, officials did not want to take any chances. They mounted tighter security on the road outside the jail, ordered random frisking of people outside, and completely prohibited the entry of visitors. Then they cut off the only link of the prisoners with the outside world that was provoking them into rebellion: they snatched away all the radio transistors.

In Kandahar, meanwhile, one of the passengers had set up a fragile link with the outside world — through the Internet. A Chinese man sitting at his home in Beijing was in an Internet chat room when another user logged on, apparently using a sophisticated satellite phone. The

Chinese man was startled by what the person who had entered the chat room had to say. Below is the transcript of the conversation, with the words as well as punctuation unchanged:

SOS SOS THE GRENADES WITH
THE HIJACKERS R NOT REAL
PLZ INFORM AUTHORITIES
I'M ON A LAPTOP
CAN'T MESSAGE AGAIN PLZ HELP

i am in china, how can i help you?
where r u?

I'm in a fuckin hijacked plane plz inform my
1st message to Indian or afghan authorities
hey u there

i am telling to my AUTHORITIES

ok go ahead plz n keep me updated

r u on the plane now?

YEAH ON A LAP TOP

I am telling to Afghanistan embassy
they said the hostage have been disimprisoned
why r u say that?

WHAT R U KIDDIN WE R 150 PEOPLE
OUT HERE

what mean "out here"

INSIDE THE PLANE

are you online now?

yah sorry got to shut 4 sometime

WHAT ABOUT NOW?
I AM TELLING TO INDIA embassy in china now
the embassy ask u what they can do for you

tell them the grenades r fake thats all

I faxing to him

ok thanxs

i have faxed

thanxs a lot ur a life saver

how many kidnapper on the plane?

5

how about u now ?
don't be afraid

well desperately need a fuckin smoke u've been
a good friend
so where r u from

the embassy ask for your real name

wait nline one is coming here
hey u there my names r k ghosh
hello plz did u get me i got just 2 mins
hello plz reply
hello plz

i know your name

ok then go ahead i'm going now thanxs 4
helping me i'll go offline r u sure the
embassy'll get it
hey u sure the embassy got it
hello

i have told them

ok bye thanxs

There was no way of knowing whether what Ghosh was saying about the grenades — that they were fake — was true. Shankar had often taken off the thin pin that acts as a lid on the upper mouth of the grenade, linked by a ring. But he held the grenade firmly in his hands, his palm pressed against an elliptical lever hanging by the side. Until the lever was pressed, it would hold a thin cylinder attached to the top of the grenade. When he did release the lever, the cylinder would strike a detonator at the bottom of the grenade which would blow up within seconds.

However, the hijackers could keep the people terrified and at the same time disarm the grenade by simply unscrewing a base plug from the bottom of the grenade.

The Chinese man faxed a printout of the conversation to the Indian embassy in Beijing, from where it was immediately faxed to India. Hours later in New Delhi, it was being circulated between curious ministers in a Cabinet meeting. Prime Minister Vajpayee started reading the note aloud. When he reached the seventh line, where Ghosh had uttered an expletive, Vajpayee stopped reading. He passed the note around.

The crimson sun was slowly disappearing behind the bleak Afghan mountains when an Indian Airlines Airbus 320 descended on the Kandahar skies, carrying a group of carefully chosen men and women who were bringing with them the only hope of saving the lives of more than 160 trapped hostages. It was 5:35 in the evening. It was the first time that Indian officials were arriving in Afghanistan after 26 September 1996 — the day the Indian embassy in Kabul was closed down in the midst of fierce fighting that resulted in the Taliban takeover. As mortar and artillery shells rained on Kabul, where the airport was closed, Indian officials had rushed to the Bagram military officials from where a planeload of Indian diplomats and other embassy staffers had fled the war-torn nation.

Three years later on a similar evening, an aircraft, smaller than the hijacked plane parked on the tarmac, was bringing a 52-member Indian team comprising of negotiators, doctors, engineers, communication personnel — and, should they be needed, commandos. It had been delayed in New Delhi due to a technical snag, and had to return after take-off. The main negotiators were Vivek Katju, a joint secretary in the ministry of foreign affairs with long years of experience in handling Pakistan matters, and Ajit Doval, a senior official in the home ministry. They were assisted by five others in the negotiating team. Inside the aircraft, Burger announced to the passengers that the Indian delegation had arrived.

The team was welcomed by a group of Taliban officials, part of a "reception committee." The negotiators immediately started consultations with Erick du Mul, the UN representative, and diplomats of other countries who had already arrived in Kandahar. The brainstorming session was over dinner. Monday's menu was meat, salad, bananas, apples and oranges.

Later the Indian officials met separately with Wakil Ahmad Muttawakil, the Taliban foreign minister. Muttawakil conveyed a message from the Amir, Mullah Omar, that the problem be resolved soon and that the Taliban would not like any bloodshed, especially during the holy month of Ramzan. In a separate newspaper interview, the Amir declared that the hijackers should either leave Afghanistan or surrender — which provoked inferences that he was calling the hijacking illegal. Despite this seemingly tough stand in the media, the Indian team found little to match the posturing on the ground. The negotiators started on an ominous note — Muttawakil cold-shouldered a proposal that Indian commandos storm the plane. He also refused to have Taliban commandos try to rescue the passengers, or even a joint operation, saying they did not have the capability to do so.

The negotiators seemed kicking against a blank wall. Even before they started negotiations, it seemed there was little to be won in Kandahar; the only hope was that the Taliban would arrest the hijackers after they were released and prosecute them according to the local law. If this was actually done strictly in accordance with Taliban law, Ibrahim Athar and his colleagues would have been whiplashed in public for their crimes — among them, being clean shaven. The Shoora would have decided the number of lashes, and then probably convicted them to be beheaded for murder.

The arrival of the Indian negotiators helped drastically reduce tension at the airport. The security cordon thrown around the aircraft in the afternoon was thinned down, and the airstrip became almost deserted apart from a few jeeps and some soldiers. Some Taliban military commanders kept watch from a distance.

Short on hope, the negotiators started on one of the toughest ever assignments at 9:45 p.m. after dinner, opening the first of several rounds of talks with the hijackers. The discussions continued late into the night, with the negotiators first trying to strike a rapport with the hijackers and trying to gauge their identity and demands. Doval was doing much of the talking. Early on in the discussions, he took the line that Erick du Mul had been taking since he came — pressing for the release of the women and children. In different words, in several different ways, the question was asked over and over again. The reply was always the same: they would be released when Azhar was freed. Chief was adamant, often rude. Sometimes, Burger or Doctor would join in the conversation. As the negotiators talked, the technicians also got to work. The relief team tried to repair the POL refuelling immobiliser. But the fault was only partly corrected in one of the engines.

On the tarmac, small groups of Taliban soldiers stood guard, wrapped in large shawls, wearing the traditional turbans and with Kalashnikov rifles slung over their shoulders. Some laid out blankets on the tarmac to rest, and to kneel at prayer time. The temperatures hovered near freezing point. Some distance away, black smoke billowed towards the dark from the small bonfires lit by the Taliban soldiers to keep themselves warm. Inside the domed airport terminal, diplomats from Switzerland, Belgium, Italy and Spain solemnly huddled together.

In New Delhi, the first rumours started doing the rounds of the press corps that the government was planning to release Masood Azhar.

DAY

5

Burger tempts ten women with an apple,
the Indian negotiators beat their heads
against a wall ... the hijackers seem to
be taking their orders from elsewhere ...

Twenty-four hours had passed by without food. Children had stopped asking questions, and the adults counselled themselves and others each time the pangs began. With shutters drawn, most of the hostages had stopped keeping track of mornings and evenings. When hunger made the children too sullen, Burger, who seemed to have a special love for them, walked up to each child one by one, talking to them about their vacations, offering them whatever sweets were left in the plane, playing little games with them and breaking into song. The hijackers remained on guard through the night but took turns to sleep, and started shouting early in the morning, asking the hostages to wake up. Some passengers were keeping notes, lest they not live to relate this horrific story. They wrote on their boarding cards, scraps of paper, even their trousers.

Then Burger stepped out of the business class with a small treasure: a large apple that had not been eaten by the hijackers. He held it in one hand — his gun in the other — and walked down the aisle shouting *"Koi ladies yahan bhookhi hain?"* (Any ladies hungry here?) Kavita Sharma, a lean young bride from New Delhi, raised her hand and Burger honoured her with the first bite. But she did not stop at one, she took three. *"Ab bas, bahut ho gaya"* (That'll be all), Burger said, as he took it away and walked further down the aisle, shouting *"Koi aur ladies ise khaengi?"* (Any other ladies want to eat this?) Within minutes, women who would have never imagined they would taste something already tasted by a stranger happily gobbled up whatever they got.

Ten women tasted that single apple. It was as if an apple-seller had walked into a plane with a horde of hungry people, and with all the riches that the passengers had, with all their money and jewellery, all that they could have had was one fruit. For those who got to taste that precious apple, it was a bite that they would probably remember for long; for those who could just watch desperately, it was a humbling experience that would haunt them at their dining tables for a long time.

Water was more precious. Since the angry hijackers had not allowed any food and water on the plane since early Monday, the bottles that Afghan children had cheerfully filled up from taps near the airport building and transported to the plane ran out over hours. Parents were asking little children to have beer from cans instead of water. Some time later, as Doctor was passing by, Kavita Sharma's husband Vishal called out to him softly and said he was very thirsty. Doctor would be remembered as different things by different people. The man who killed Ripan Katyal could be sensitive and empathetic at times, he could even sound deeply religious at times. He told Vishal: *"Yaar, paani to khatam ho gaya lagta hai, par dekhte hain"* (It seems the water is over, but let's see in the front). Then he walked to the front rows, looked around, and came back after a few minutes. *"Aage ki rows ke paas kuchch soda bottles hain. Unhe le aao par dekhna ki koi aur na dekh le"* (There are a few soda bottles near the front rows. Go and get them, but see that no one watches you bring them). The last thing the hijackers would have wanted on the plane was a water riot.

Meanwhile, there were other emergencies they would have to deal with. At about 9:30 a.m., the lights in the plane suddenly went off. The scared passengers heard a loud, unusual whirring noise at the back. Nothing could have been worse for the already desperate passengers. The cooling system seemed to have been affected, because the air conditioning started shutting down. It became cold. Frightened sighs swept through the plane. There were Taliban commandos around the plane in three cars — one near the left wing, one below the aircraft's tail and the other below the nose. The Taliban guards below the plane's tip heard the loud noise, and immediately reported it to the officials at the airport. Engineers were consulted. The Indian delegation was informed, and the control tower in turn told Chief in the cockpit what had happened: The plane's auxilliary power unit had shut down.

It was a sunny morning. The doors of the aircraft were opened to let some fresh air into the stench-soaked aircraft. After throwing tantrums for a day, the hijackers relented and also asked for food. A step ladder was brought to the plane and a guard walked up around noon with large black plastic bags, one stuffed with rotis and the other with daal (pulses) in separate packets. The food was delivered. For some time, the passengers did not understand what had gone wrong with the aircraft. The auxiliary power unit near the tail of the aircraft provides air-conditioning while the plane is on the ground, and is also used to provide air pressure to start the engines. A jet engine has to rotate at approximately a fifth of its highest attainable speed before the fuel supply begins and the engine roars to a start. If the APU failed, the aircraft would have no electrical supply and it would be pitch dark inside the plane, with the shutters already drawn.

An Indian engineer needed to go inside the plane to inspect the unit, but the hijackers refused to allow anyone on board. After some persuasion and quibbling, Chief agreed to send out one of the hijackers as guarantee for the engineer's security. Columns of cameras rolled and clicked as Doctor stepped out of the plane wearing a black mask, red T-shirt and trousers with large black checks, offering to the front pages of the world's newspapers the next morning the first sight of the hijackers. He remained outside for about thirty minutes, first standing near the plane, and then walked to sit in a jeep nearby, with a portly, bearded Taliban official watching over him and an Indian official a little far away. Inside the plane, engineer R.K. Sharma worked under frightening circumstances — one hijacker held a gun to his head and the other to his abdomen. Sharma saw some passengers playing cards, others reading newspapers — news that would pacify their desperate relatives back home.

Across the tarmac in the control tower, Katju, Doval and the rest of the negotiating team continued their tedious discussions with the hijackers. The fact that they were getting nowhere despite two days of talks made the hijackers irritable and furious. *"Sharm aani chahiye! Tumhari government ko tumhari pareshani ki koi fiqr nahin hai"* (Shame on you! Your government doesn't care about your suffering), Burger shouted at the Indian passengers. Soon after the hijackers told the passengers that an official of the delegation would come inside the plane. Passengers were not to speak with him; they would be shot if they did. The hostages would wait all day in hope.

Both sides had more or less stuck to their own during the nightlong talks. In the morning, the Indian side gave one more try to raising the issue of Rachna Katyal. They requested the hijackers to release her as a humanitarian gesture, an appeal repeated several times on television and in newspapers by the Katyal family.

"Hum aapko batayenge" (We will tell you in a while), Chief said. About thirty minutes later, they returned to the conversation, and refused to free Rachna — confirming the negotiators' doubts that the hijackers were taking instructions from elsewhere, and the orders now were to be unyielding in the negotiations. *"Is tarah masoom logon se salooq karna Islam ke khilaaf hai"* (This mistreatment of innocent people is against Islam), Doval tried to reason. This infuriated Chief. *"Hamein Islam sikhane ki koshish mat karo"* (Don't try to teach us Islam), he snapped.

The negotiations were extremely difficult for the Indian officials, but they were no less taxing for Chief as well. According to Capt. Sharan, Chief cried on his shoulders at least three times during the duration they were in Kandahar, frustrated with the slow pace of the negotiations. For him, the talks finally seemed to be getting somewhere when they were asked for the full list of their demands around noon.

Chief and his men got to work. For the next few hours, they mulled over their demands. So far the hijackers had only been demanding Azhar and "several of our brothers" — now they had to give names and details about the men. Indian investigators believe that the hijackers made calls to Karachi during this period to someone who had a comprehensive list of Islamic militants imprisoned in Indian jails, along with names of their fathers, for quick identification.

Then Chief got stuck. He wanted to ask the Indian side to have the body of a dead militant exhumed from his grave and handed over to them. But he did not know how to say that in English. Burger thought of one person who would certainly know. He stepped out of the cockpit and walked to the only American woman among the hostages — Jeanne Moore, fifty-three, of Bakersfield, California. Moore, a psychotherapist and a special education teacher at the Kern County Child Development Center, was probably one hostage who could have helped out all the stressed out people around her, including the hijackers. Moore had been in Kathmandu because of her love for vacationing in far-flung locations. The hijackers had already snatched her passport after they came to know of her identity, and had also turned down her offer that she speak with the US government for help on the issue. Despite the hijackers' supposed respect for women, she was among the people attacked by them — when she moved suddenly as she tried to blow off a bug from her hand, she got a whack on the head. In an aircraft whose over-used air conditioning system made the cabins too hot or too cold, she had already contracted pneumonia. She had been living in constant terror that as an American citizen, she would be an obvious target for killing and applying pressure on the Indian government — if all of them were not killed from a grenade or in a shootout. She had only prayed that the death be quick and painless. Now, Burger was going to say something that would make her believe that that moment had finally arrived.

"What do you call the box in which they keep a body?" Burger asked her. Moore's first thought was that it was for her. Nevertheless, she told Burger: "Coffin. C-O-F-F-I-N." Then she wrote it on a slip of paper and gave it to him. Burger walked into the cockpit and copied the word onto the list Chief was preparing for the negotiators.

Soon the list written in English in long hand on white paper was ready. It would shake up authorities in New Delhi: it demanded the release of Maulana Masood Azhar; release of thirty-five other militants whose details were given; two hundred million US dollars in ransom, and the coffin of Sajjad Afghani, Azhar's dear friend and jail mate who was killed during a failed jailbreak attempt in Jammu's Kot Bhalwal jail several months earlier. The list was thrown out of the plane and a Taliban soldier standing nearby carried it to the control tower. Thirty-three of the thirty-six prisoners were Pakistanis.

Prime Minister Vajpayee got busy in an urgent meeting in New Delhi as soon as one of the negotiators called up officials in New Delhi on a satellite phone and informed them of the demand. The war of nerves had entered a crucial phase.

Within an hour, dozens of policemen mounted a vigil outside the Gujjarnagar graveyard in Jammu, a few hundred metres away from the official residence of Chief Minister Farooq Abdullah. Sajjad Afghani lay there in an inconspicuous grave covered with shrubs, and Chief had demanded that the body be exhumed from the grave and handed over to him.

The release of Masood Azhar was the ultimate aim of the hijackers, but the death of Sajjad Afghani was the immediate provocation. It had to be avenged. The tall and hefty Afghani, whose real name was Sajjad Khan, was very special for Maulana Masood Azhar. They had been together after Azhar came to Srinagar and were arrested together. They had stayed in the same barracks at the Kot Bhalwal prison.

Azhar wrote a glowing account of Afghani and his feelings for him in a letter to Afghani's parents a few months after the death of their son:

"A month ago a lawyer who used to visit both of us came to see me. He was surprised to find me all alone. I told him everything and begged him to go to Gujjarnagar in Jammu, to the mazaar-e-shahada (grave of the martyr) there, offer dua at Sajjad Shaheed's grave and bring back a photograph of it for me. Maybe my restless soul could find some peace. A few days ago I received the photograph. The sight of his grave tearfully refreshed his memories, still fresh in my heart.

"Memories come crowding upon me. I have so much to tell you. But before writing anything else I want to tell you that after Sajjad Khan's shahada I gathered together all his belongings and kept them with me, tied in a bundle, for many days. There was no way I could contact you and ask you for your permission for their disposal, for you were the legal heirs. Among his possessions were sixteen hundred rupees, his clothes, shoes, a radio set, etc. Giving up hope of ever being able to contact you, I at last after istikhara and consultation with the other companions, distributed them among the mujahideen as sadaqaah.

"I used to dream that I would attend his wedding and as the qazi deliver his marriage sermon. I sometimes mentioned this to Sajjad and I think he enjoyed it but my small hopes were not destined to come true... In His Divine Mercy (Allah) took Sajjad out of the prison and made him a guest of his own. Instead of marrying him to some mortal woman of this world Allah Ta'ala married him to the hoors of Jannat... Had he been set free from the prison here, had he got married, no one knows how long his happiness might have lasted. But that which you have now received is permanent and lasting until eternity.

"Today Islam has fallen upon such distressing times. The qafirs of the whole world are trying to efface Islam and the Muslims from the face of the earth. The irony is that the Muslims themselves, out of greed for this world, have pushed out Islam from their homes... Your son has been fortunate enough to sacrifice his life for upholding Islam in its days of need and poverty.

"Millions of blessings of Allah Ta'ala are upon him who even in prison could never be subjugated. Not for a single moment did he bow down to his captors. They beat him, tortured him till they got tired but he untiringly proclaimed the supremacy of Islam... Just before his shahada a new officer was appointed. He was an expert in the techniques of torture and knew how to subdue even the most recalcitrant prisoner, it was said. He had been sent to our prison with the sole purpose of breaking us down. On the very first day of his arrival he entered our prison ward and thundered: "Fall in line, each one of you. I want to count the roll."

"Sajjad sahib rose up from behind and called out: 'You son of a mushrik who are you to make us stand in a line? There is none born of a mother who can make us Muslims

[125]

fall into lines.' So threatening was Sajjad's figure that the officer started trembling.

"I was very anxious to have his funeral rites performed in accordance with Sharia'ah. I could do nothing except pray to Allah Ta'ala and put some pressure upon the prison officials. Alhamdulillah.

"Allah Ta'ala's help descended. The doctor who performed his post-mortem was a Muslim. He himself saw a glow of light, a noor emanating from the shaheed's body. Then an acquaintance of Sajjad Sahib, who was also the brother of a mujahid associate, by chance heard the news of Sajjad's shahada and he managed to persuade the police into handing over the body to him... The shaheed's body was then carried to a masjid of Jammu ..."

If the government did give in to the hijackers and agree to the swap of hostages for militants, it would not be the first time it would be doing so. One such deal, the December 1989 release of five Kashmiri militants for Rubaiya Sayeed, the daughter of the then Home Minister Mufti Mohammad Sayeed, had became a point of reference for the angry relatives of the hostages on board IC-814. Today, it figured in the negotiations as well and the hijackers mentioned the hostage-for-militants swap several times. Sayeed's release during the regime of the then Prime Minister Vishwanath Pratap Singh inspired a string of abductions.Two years later, Naheed Soz, daughter of the then National Conference leader Saifuddin Soz, was abducted and later released in exchange for a dreaded militant. The next year, in January 1992, a similar deal was struck to set free Tassadaq Dev, the brother-in-law of the then Parliamentary Affairs Minister Ghulam Nabi Azad, who was abducted by members of the Al Umar Mujahideen group. In exchange, three jailed militants were released. Six militants were released in exchange for hostage K. Doraiswamy, the executive director of the Indian Oil Corporation.

Despite the precedents, the hijackers had now made an outrageous demand in Kandahar, although it could be a bargaining ploy. The negotiations were now in a crucial phase, and Taliban officials also started taking an active part in the talks, almost becoming a third party in the discussions, and almost always seeming to side with the hostage-takers.

With the hijackers and the Taliban both mounting pressure, it seemed a matter of time before the negotiators would be boxed into a corner on an impossible turf. But Doval and Katju tried to delay that situation as far as possible. They argued that officials did not know which jails the militants demanded by the hijackers were lodged in, even predicting a situation where the government could be ready to release the militants but their release could get bogged down in court wrangles.

Chief retorted: "*Jo poochha jaye uska jawab deejiye. Apne jawab chhote rakhiye, aur bataiye ki kya aap hamare saathiyon ko chhorenge ya nahin?*" (Answer to the point, keep your answers short and tell us will you release our friends or not?). After long quibbling, the hijackers seemed to be ready to release all the women children, old and sick people in return for Masood Azhar.

Meanwhile, Taliban cleaners entered the plane once again to rid the aircraft of some of its ever-growing stench. The cleaners opened the pipes of the aircraft's toilets from the outside. On the verge of desperation, several passengers burst into tears on seeing the men. But tension was growing, and the hijackers did not trust anyone, not even their hosts. Ever alert to the possibility of commandos in disguise coming on the plane, the hijackers lined up the cleaners and frisked them. The hijackers ordered the cleaning staff not to move around in the plane and prohibited them from speaking with any passenger, or staying inside the aircraft for more than an hour. Among the trash they collected were clothes with old, clotted stains of Ripan Katyal's blood.

One door of the aircraft was open, as the air conditioning unit had so far not been rectified. The hostages had a very cold night ahead of them.

In the Bush House, London, a staff reporter picked up the phone as the bell rang in the office of the Urdu radio service of the British Broadcasting Corporation. The call was from India, from Bombay, and the man at the other end was Abdul Latif, the main accomplice of Ibrahim Athar. He had just received a call from Karachi from Abdul Rauf, younger brother of Maulana Masood Azhar and Ibrahim Athar. Rauf understood the importance of the media in a situation like this: he asked Latif to call up journalists and convey a threat on behalf of the hijackers.

"*Main* Indian Airlines plane *kee* hijacking *ke silsile mein bol raha hoon*" (I am calling in connection with the Indian Airlines hijacking), Latif said. "*Aap batayen ki fidayeen ka* message *hai, agar maulana ko chaubees ghante ke andar release nahin kiya gaya, to jahaz uda diya jaega*" (Broadcast a message from the suicide fighters: if the maulana is not released within twenty-four hours, the plane will be blown up).

In another part of the city, someone had been keeping a close watch on both of Latif's phone calls. For the intelligence officials tracking him for days, this call would prove to be the clincher.

It was another night when Flight Engineer Jaggia would not be able to sleep in peace. At about 2:30 a.m., he was woken up by Burger. He was needed to supervise the refilling of water from a Russian tanker parked outside. It was a very cold night, and Jaggia was wearing just his shirt. He shivered as he tried to connect the water hose to an opening for water, but the mouth of the hose was too big. The strong current of water gushed in and Jaggia was totally drenched in a second. He started shivering badly.

Burger took off his leather jacket and offered it to Jaggia, still pointing his gun at the flight engineer with the other hand. It was one of those moments of the puzzling emotional bonds between the hijackers and the same frightened people they were threatening to kill.

"*Aap mere* father *ki tarah hain. Main aapko thand mein marte nahin dekh sakta hoon*" (You are like my father, I don't want to see you die like this), Burger told Jaggia, who was now shaking in the cold.

"*Agar main pita ki tarah hoon to apne bete ko bhi aise sirf* T-shirt *pehen kar is thand mein khare nahin dekh sakta. Jaldi se jacket pehen lo*" (If I am like your father, even I can't see you standing in this cold wearing just a T-shirt. Put on your jacket), he said firmly.

Burger meekly complied, but pulled Jaggia away to an airport authority Land Rover parked nearby. He opened the door and ordered the driver to put the heat on full blast, but warned Jaggia not to talk to the Taliban technician sitting inside. After about thirty minutes, Burger returned. Jaggia was dry, and both walked back to the plane. Burger once again put a gun to Jaggia's head.

"*Yaar kis matti ke bane ho? Na jeene dete ho, na marne dete ho*" (What are you made of? You neither let me live, nor let me die), Jaggia said as he smiled.

Burger replied calmly: "*Vo bhi* duty *hai, yeh bhi* duty *hai*"
(That is also my duty, this is also my duty).

DAY

6

Relatives of passengers resort to faith — but it's not clear whose side God is on ... the Mumbai Crime Branch zeroes in on a prime suspect ... and the Indian government reconciles itself to releasing militants

It was 1:15 in the morning. Ibrahim Athar's sharp, angry voice rang out across the aircraft. The fatigued passengers woke up with a start. "_Maulana ka masla pehle hal hoga phir kuchch aur hoga_" (First Masood Azhar's issue will be settled, and only then anything else can happen), Athar was snapping at the Indian negotiators. Chief had mishandled the communication equipment inside the cockpit, going on the public address system even while he thought he was speaking to the negotiators. For the passengers, it was only a chilling reminder that even after spending five days in oblivion, they had got nowhere and there were no real prospects of their release so far. The negotiators had told the hijackers that the answer to their extravagant demands was 'no'. They had also rejected the hijackers' offer to release ten Indians and five foreigners if Masood was freed. For their part, the hijackers opened the day's talks by refusing to honour their commitment made the previous evening to free all women, children, the old and the sick, in exchange for Masood Azhar. Things seemed set for a long haul.

In New Delhi, in a large room with a huge circular table and a small chandelier inside the red sandstone South Block office of Prime Minister Vajpayee, senior ministers were seated for a Cabinet meeting. Intelligence reports from across the country were pointing to the build-up of tense religious rivalries between Hindus and Muslims in many places. There was a real possibility of religious clashes over the hijacking. Dozens of journalists had assembled outside the building flanked by the opulent Rashtrapati Bhavan in the background. As the meeting ended, the ministers briskly walked out of the Cabinet room and got into their cars without speaking to the journalists. Parliamentary Affairs Minister Pramod Mahajan, a man who has many friends in the media, was mobbed by reporters as he emerged from the meeting. He would say nothing of the discussions; only that India's response to their demands had been conveyed to the hijackers. He indicated a tough line on the talks, and called it "a battle of patience."

But patience was becoming a very precious quality. It was in short supply all over — across the country in the homes of the hostages; inside the plane where the hijackers were barking threats every few hours to kill the passengers or blow up the plane; among the Taliban, which had played the good host for too long; and the fatigued Indian negotiators. The new demands brandished by the hijackers had stunned the relatives of the hostages. They were too numb to react. After staging violent protests for days and slamming the government for doing very little, they withdrew into the sadness of their homes, reconciling themselves to what now seemed inevitable. The daily protests outside the prime minister's house stopped. No furious relatives stormed a press conference. They did not lie down on the streets to stop traffic or weep in public or beat their chests or abuse the officials or jostle with the police. They were now left with only one weapon.

Prayer.

Navneet Kaur, wife of Capt. Sharan, drove to a religious gathering at Gurudwara Tikana Sahib in New Delhi along with dozens of other relatives of the hostages. A white shawl draped over her shoulders, she covered her face with her hands as tears welled in her eyes. Other women watched in sombre silence as the large hall hummed with prayers. In hundreds of temples across the country, people were similarly praying for the hostages. Religious leaders of the Hindu, Jain, Muslim, Sikh and Christian faiths offered to go to Kandahar to talk to the hijackers. Even a radical Muslim group, the Jamaat-e-Islami Hind, criticised the hijacking and urged the hijackers to release the hostages. Its chief suggested the hijackers adopt other means to get their demands fulfilled.

Across the Indian Ocean in the Australian city of Melbourne, another small group was joining in prayer. Sachin Tendulkar, captain of the Indian cricket team took some moments in the dressing room in the midst of the second Test against Australia to lead his teammates in special prayers for the release of the passengers.

In the aircraft as well, both the hijackers and the hostages were resorting to faith — but there seemed little agreement on whose side God was on. Doctor, the man who knew the most on religion among the five hijackers and said he had done research on religion, was giving a speech on Islam on the public address system.

"*Hum aapke saath badsalooqi nahin kar rahe hain. Aaj tak humne jo bhi seekha hai aur jo bhi kiya hai, vo Islam ki badaulat kiya hai. Hum jo hain, vo Islam ki khatir hain. Agar aapko lagta hai ki hum aapse koi zyadti kar rahe hain ya humne koi galtiyan ki hain, to ye sirf isliye hai ki humne Islam ko theek tarah parha nahin, use seekha nahin*" (We are not misbehaving with you. Islam has taught us to be what we are, to do what we do. We owe everything to Islam. If you think we have hurt you or made some mistakes, it is only because we have not been good students of Islam).

Doctor also spoke on other worldly matters. "UNO *ko sirf Chechnya ki fiqr hai, vo* Kashmir *ke liye kuchch nahin kar rahe hain jahan par Hindustani security forces barbadi phaila rahe hain*" (The UN is worried only about Chechnya, they are not doing anything about Kashmir where Indian security forces are wrecking the land), he thundered.

"*Hamare bhai chheh-saat baras se Hindustan ki jailon mein sar rahe hain. Hamari behnon ko Hindustani sipahi* rape *kar rahe hain. Vo Hindustani unko unke gharon se jaanwaron ki tarah baal se pakar kar ghaseetate hain*" (Our brothers are rotting in jail for six-seven years. Our sisters are raped by Indian soldiers. The Indians pull them out of their houses like animals, pulling their hair).

Burger understood popular taste better. When he was not terrifying people, he seemed to specialise in public relations. Sometimes he would walk into the passenger cabins in an extremely tense moment, and lighten up the atmosphere in just a few seconds with a joke or a song. It seemed part of a well-planned psychological game to keep the passengers from getting too desperate due to the terror of the other hijackers. But for desperate passengers

[134]

wavering almost each hour between hope and despair, he was the perfect respite from his associates. Most passengers would later remember Burger fondly.

One such man was the father of two, a boy and girl, who broke down before Burger as he told him of his children. Burger took a piece of paper and wrote for the son. The message, written in English with a blue ball point pen, was in bold longhand writing: "My dearest son, when you see your father, respect him ..." Burger was the only hijacker who cared to speak about himself and his background. In personal conversations, he told the hostages he had graduated in science and had done an engineering course — though passengers doubted this when he later asked basic things about a generator that engineers normally know, like the conversion of amperes into volts. He also mentioned his new-born daughter to several passengers, and said she was special because she was born after his wife suffered several miscarriages.

In a moment of camaraderie, Dr. Lalit Varma of Gurgaon shook his hand and said: "*Aapke haath bade soft hain*" (Your hands are very soft). Burger replied, straight-faced: "*Mera dil bhi bada soft hai par waqt aane par main bada tough ho sakta hoon*" (I have a soft heart as well but I can be cruel when the time comes).

Today, in a break from the terror hours, Burger had organised a medley of songs, Antakshari. There were two teams — the married couples versus the others. Four songs later, one side started singing the peppy Hindi film song "*Yamma Yamma, Yamma, Yamma, Yeh khoobsurat sama/Bas aaj ki rat hai zindagi, kal tum kahan hum kahan...*" When the participants reached the second line — which meant "There is life only tonight, God knows where we will be tomorrow" — the voices became hushed and died down, and the

[135]

passengers looked at each other with meaningful glances. There was too much of an autobiographical note in the song. Then Burger broke the silence: *"Arre sirf aaj ki raat kyon hai bhai zindagi?"* (Why do you say there is life only tonight?)

When not having their subdued fun, the hostages plotted an escape. The crew members got some moments with the passengers between trips to the toilet or during the distribution of food, and in these moments they were engaged in playing a little game of Chinese whispers: if the hijackers started killing the passengers on board or if the aircraft was stormed, the crew wanted the passengers to be prepared. Crew members spread the word that if the commander shouted "Evacuate!" the passengers would open the emergency exits and jump off the aircraft. Though a large number would possibly be injured and some could die in a shooting, the rest could survive. But such a plan could also prove foolhardy because the hostages were unsure whose side the Taliban commandos standing outside would take in such a situation.

On Wednesday, Taliban soldiers stood guard on the tarmac, their heads wrapped in bulky turbans. Once every few hours they laid out their blankets and offered their prayers, some bowing beneath the wing of the parked aircraft. They huddled for warmth on the wind-swept runway near small bonfires. Temperatures had fallen below zero the previous night and it was still very cold.

In New Delhi, Anthea Mulakala was waiting for her husband on their fourth wedding anniversary on 29 December in New Delhi, at the plush residence of an Australian diplomat. In all probability, he would not make it — Peter Ward, thirty-six, was among the hostages in the plane in Kandahar. Ward is an Australian and his wife holds British and Canadian citizenships. Mulakala had come to New Delhi from Bangladesh, where she works, to join her Nepal-based husband, a credit manager for Grindlays Nepal Bank, for a vacation that would pack in Christmas, the anniversary and the New Year.

For the hijackers, the first climbdown came in the afternoon. There seemed no way the Indian government would give in to the demand for thirty militants and two hundred million dollars, and until they kept insisting that all their demands be met, things got nowhere. But the Taliban, also getting weary of the hijacking drama, began to apply pressure on both sides. Taliban representative Rehmatullah Hashmi and the corps commander for Kandahar, Akhtar Mohmmed Usmani, were now in the control tower, talking to the hijackers along with the Indian officials. Later Muttawakil also walked in. He told the hijackers that the demand for the money and the dead body was against Islam. There was debate. Finally, Chief agreed to scale down the demands. There would be no money sought now, and Afghani would remain where he was — in the Jammu graveyard.

Over the next few hours, there was another broad agreement reached. The hijackers agreed to release thirty-five passengers, mostly women, children and sick people, in return for Masood Azhar. The exact procedure of the release still had to be worked out. Muttawakil told the hijackers that they as well as the released prisoner would not step on Afghan soil, and that the Pakistan consulate would send its vehicle to the airport to take them away. He then left the control tower, apparently to ask Pakistani officials if they agreed with this arrangement. The hijackers were hopeful the agreement would be implemented by the evening. In the passenger cabin, they started segregating thirty-five passengers as well. Each of these passengers was asked to pick up their hand baggage from the mounds of bags thrown in the business class. There was some chaos: several passengers saw this as their last chance of freedom. One man's wife was asked to get up and walk to the business class; he had a bout of hysteria. He stiffened up, started howling and shook violently. *"Mujhe jaane do! Mujhe jaane do!"* (Let me go! Let me go!), he screamed. His wife consoled him, asked him to calm down. Then the hijackers relented and asked him also to go to the business class.

Burger shouted to the rest of the passengers, who were watching helplessly: *"Koi* message *bhejna chahta hai?* Phone number *aur* message *de deejiye"* (Anyone wants to send a message home? Give the phone number and message), he said. There was a rush to write small notes on scraps of paper. Ramesh Grover would remember exactly what he wrote in the message: his telephone number at his New Delhi residence, and the words: "So far so good. See you soon if we get out." Burger collected the telephone numbers and the messages, to be handed over to the people being released.

Finally, the talks seemed to be progressing, and zeroed in on the main demand: the thirty-six militants. Now the Taliban also tried to apply pressure on the Indian side. Muttawakil declared that the Taliban would force the plane to take off from Kandahar. The Taliban's highest decision-making body, the Shoora, went into session that night. Aware of a meeting between Prime Minister Vajpayee and the chiefs of India's army, air force and navy, the Taliban leaders were concerned that New Delhi might try an Entebbe-style raid to free the hostages. Mullah Omar and the Shoora made one key decision that was aimed at New Delhi: No foreign power, a reference to India, would be allowed to launch a commando raid to free the hostages. An Entebbe-style storming was ruled out.

An ocean of people was pouring into Mumbai's Mohammad Ali Road. It was the holy month of Ramzan, the day's fasting was over, and there was shopping to be done. A hundred hawkers screamed in a dissonant chorus, begging people to buy everything from colourful children's frocks with frills, to jaggery and packets of soiled dates. Men, women and children filled up every possible centimetre of space in an unending torrent. Unknown to all others, a small group of men were going to carry out an impossible task. They had to keep watch over one man — just one man — in an ever-surging crowd of hundreds, possibly thousands, that was madly jostling, walking, driving, honking horns, flailing arms. Officers and sharpshooters of the Crime Branch had descended on Mohammad Ali Road that evening — in the neon lights, they had to track down Abdul Latif, the main accomplice of Ibrahim Athar. The officers were all in plain clothes. Latif was the man receiving messages and instructions from Abdul Rauf in Karachi, and passing them on to the hijackers when they called him from inside the plane. He had kept the hijackers informed of all that was going on outside the plane, from the angry protests of the relatives to the dilemma of the government.

Latif was the link that could lead investigators to the hijackers. The Crime Branch had been tipped off that Latif would meet a contact in a small restaurant in the Mohammad Ali market, who would hand him a bag. As the officers spread out, it was getting dark, and it began to seem that their man had slipped away. A lone man could have dissolved into the surge of people in a second — the crowd was so much that it could have probably sucked in a train of horses as well and made them disappear. Then, the sleuths standing outside the small restaurant saw a lean man in T-shirt and jeans sitting with another man. The man in the jeans seemed to match the description of Latif, but the detectives were not sure. A few minutes later, a bag changed hands. The officers got ready — though still unsure if they had the right man. The officers took their chance. As Latif stepped out of the restaurant, he was followed. It was an impossible chase that any detective could be proud of — just following a head bobbing up and down in a sea of other heads. On their walkie-talkies, the senior officer ordered other men to fan out in the locality. It took several men to keep track of Latif as he went down the road and into smaller bylanes, walking for a long time in the dark before he briskly climbed up the stairs of a seven-storey building near a large shantytown in the Jogeshwari neighbourhood. He climbed right up to the fourth floor.

As Latif went to sleep a few hours later, there were other men who would have to be awake all night. Crime Branch officers were to keep a nightlong vigil outside the building. There was work to be done in the morning.

Even for politicians who are used to haggling for constituencies and ministries in an era of coalition politics, the deal-making was in a tough stage. Prime Minister Vajpayee sat listening to senior ministers and top advisers at his residence late on Wednesday, mulling the consequences of agreeing to the hijackers' demands as well as refusing them. With the hijackers threatening to force the aircraft out of Kandahar, the government considred the possible destinations of the hijackers. The number of countries which could harbour the hijackers was limited. Officials zeroed in on Libya and Sudan. Foreign Minister Jaswant Singh, who did most of the talking, told the Cabinet that the Libyan foreign minister had assured him of all assistance if the plane headed its way. Which left Sudan — and civil aviation authorities soon confirmed that with replenished fuel tanks, the plane could directly fly the 3,200 nautical miles (5,920 kilometers) to the Sudanese capital of Khartoum. That would hack away even the tiny control over the situation that the Indians had now. It was a precarious and dangerous situation.

Even if the plane did not leave Kandahar, it was hard to decide what would be more disastrous — releasing militants caught with great effort by soldiers, or watching helplessly as the hard-to-crack hijackers harmed the passengers. They decided to take the route of minimum losses in the impossible circumstances they were now facing: release Masood Azhar in return for all the hostages.

The hijackers did not agree. They wanted more. They worked on their own mathematics: Azhar's price would be eighty hostages. For each of the remaining militants whose release they wanted, fifteen hostages would be freed. This would mean the freedom of Azhar and twelve other militants. The negotiators refused. Chief refused to talk. After some steps forward, the negotiators and the hijackers had gone backward.

Several hours after the thirty-five passengers were separated for release, they were quickly shunted back to their seats.

Doctor was screaming. "*Tumhare* Indian negotiator *bekar hain. Tum mar rahe ho aur vo* shopping *karne gaye hain. Vo kaju, badam khareed rahe hain"* (Your Indian negotiators are useles. You are dying and they have gone shopping. They are buying dry fruits in Kabul). The thirty-five passengers in the business class were shifted back to their seats. Hopes fell. Many women started weeping, and Burger told them: *"Main ek Musalman hoon. Aap royen mat. Main vada karta hoon sari behne sahee salamat ghar pahunch jayengi. Ye Hindustan ki jhoothi sarkar ka vada nahin hai. Ye ek Musalmaan ka vada hai"* (I am a Muslim. Please do not cry. I promise you that all sisters will go home safely. This is not the false promise of the Indian government. This is the word of a Mussalman).

But he could not keep the hopes up for long. Two more hours passed, and the passengers were drifting off to sleep, when there was a breakdown in talks inside the cockpit. The haggling had dragged on, with no side relenting. Neither side agreed on anything. Chief decided he would have to show his mettle. With the bitterness and acrimony now, both sides were worse off than where they stood on 24 December. The hijackers were furious. In a shrill and desperate parting comment, Chief said: *"Hum tayyare ko bum se uda denge aur tum saari mauton ke liye zimmedar hoge"* (We will blow up the plane and you will be responsible for the deaths of all the passengers).

The hijackers rushed out of the cockpit. With a handheld microphone, Burger started shouting to people to wake up. *"Tum sab so rahe ho aur yahan tumhari jaan par bani hui hai. Utho!"* (All of you are sleeping here, when your lives are at stake. Wake up!). He gave bad news: *"Baatcheet naqamyaab ho gayee hai. Ab hun aur intezaar nahin kar sakte. Kal subah hum aap subko maarna shuroo kar denge"* (Talks have failed. Now we cannot wait any longer. Tomorow morning we will start killing people).

As word reached New Delhi of the new developments and the fiercely aggressive stance of the hijackers, there seemed very little the government could now hope for. The public stance remained tough and steely, but Prime Minister Vajpayee and his closest colleagues had reconciled themselves to the release of some militants. It was only a matter of working out the specifics of the swap.

DAY

7

==

*There's good news for passengers at last — a deal has
been struck for their release ... and after seven days of
living with Burger, they finally get to eat one. In Mumbai,
a key accomplice of the hijackers is arrested*

T he wake-up call came at 5:40, though hardly anyone
had slept through the night. Carrying microphones in their
hands, Burger, Shankar and Bhola walked down the aisles,
shouting at people to get up. After several days during
which there had been phases of laughter, jokes and songs,
the hijackers seemed to have reverted to being the same
ruthless men who had terrified them at gunpoint seven
days ago. Their bodies aching with pain and anxiety, the
passengers got up and sat straight in their seats. Flanked
by three other hijackers, all carrying their weapons, Burger
had an announcement to make.

"*Hamein ek* announcement *karna hai. Dhyan se suno. Ye
achchi khabar bhi ho sakti hai aur buri khabar bhi*" (We have to

[144]

make an announcement. Listen carefully. This could be either good news or bad news), he said. Then the hijackers said their prayers.

"*Hindustan ki sarkar aur hamare beech baatcheet chal rahee thi. Ab baatcheet naqamyaab ho gayee hai. Hamara unse koi raafta nahin hai. Vo hamari koi bhi* demand *maanne ko tayyar nahin hain. Ab humse rehem ki ummeed mat rakhna*" (Discussions were going on between us and the Indian government. Now the talks have broken down. There is no contact between us and them. They are not ready to accept any of our demands. Now do not expect mercy from us), he said grimly.

"*Hum kab tak tumhe baitha ke khila sakte hain? Bahut maza ho gaya*" (How long can we feed you? You have had enough fun), Burger said.

A few passengers sighed in shock. A few muted sobs were heard. Within a few seconds, there was total silence in the plane. Then one man gathered courage and spoke out: "*Hamein* negotiators *se baat karne den*" (Please let us talk to the Indian negotiators).

Burger shouted: "Shut up!" After a few minutes, he delivered the death sentence that the hijackers had decided on: "*Aaj aapki zindagi ka aakhri din hai. Ek baje hum aapko marna shuroo kar denge. Hum aage se shuroo karenge aur peechhe tak marte jaenge. Apne apne khuda ko dua kar lo*" (Today is the last day of your life. At one o'clock, we will start shooting you. We will start at the front and shoot each row until we reach the back. Pray to your Gods).

No one dared speak after that, but a Punjabi-speaking woman in the back rows muttered loudly enough for her neighbours to hear: "*Asi to mar jayenge par inse chimar jaenge!*" (We will die but before that we will swarm and attack these people).

It was a moment beyond words. After seven horrific and uncertain days spent teetering between tears and slaps and smiles and revolver butts and jokes and songs and threats and assurances, it finally seemed that the final moment had come. The hijackers had never seemed more determined, never more ruthless. They put pistols to some passengers' heads. The last few days had given the hostages hope that maybe they could survive this imprisonment and get back alive to their homes to tell the story they would pass on to their grandchildren.

But they were now facing death — and it ripped their hearts because it was not instantaneous, it was not as if the hijackers had blown them to smithereens in one brief moment of agony. They had been told the time they would be killed, and it was still about seven hours away. They would spend these long hours imagining in the most grotesque of ways how each of them would be killed, how row upon row of people would shriek and topple lifeless on their seats in small puddles of blood as others watched in the seconds before they themselves would be ripped by the bullets and the shrapnel. It was a moment that they would be scared to think of for the rest of their lives. Their tragic circumstances had brought them to the most degraded state that anyone could possibly be in.

They had not brushed their teeth for a week. Several terrified passengers — women as well as men — had passed urine sitting on their seats as they imagined their imminent death. They sat in their wet saris and trousers, their neighbours horrified and yet amused. Several fainted. Others threw up, spraying their seats and the floor with vomit. Almost all were either crying or wanted badly to cry. Many trembled so badly that their bodies could be seen shaking. As they trembled, they closed their eyes tightly and prayed.

One woman clutched on hard to her faith, though her face was ashen with terror and drenched in tears. Kavita Sharma was crying horribly but she still turned to her husband and said: "*Mujhe abhi bhi vishwas hai. Mujhe abhi bhi vishwas hai. Hum ghar jaenge aur New Year par Kalkaji mein honge*" (I am still hopeful. I am still hopeful. We will go home. We will be in Kalkaji on New Year's day).

Another woman gently approached the hijackers once with a letter to her daughter that she had written days ago, and which she had been trying to give to Burger or Doctor since. She wanted it to be passed on to her little daughter if she herself was killed with her husband on board. The hijackers had refused to take the letter so far. "*Koi fayda nahin hai*" (There is no point), one of the hijackers told her. "*Agar aap log nahin rahenge to hum bhi nahin rahenge*" (There's no point. If you die, we would be dead as well). She persisted, and finally Burger took it. Burger, screaming at passengers until some minutes ago, cried as he read the simple words.

Samant Barara of New Delhi had a stomach ailment that he described to the hijackers as stomach cancer — though other doctors later said it was a ploy to get out of the plane. The hijackers asked Barara to sit in the spacious business class seats, and he saw the hijackers huddled in discussions on what they would do next. From the stray words he caught, he guessed that they were deciding whether to blow up the plane or shoot to kill. Barara, twenty-five, was later allowed to go out of the aircraft for treatment at a hospital forty kilometres from Kandahar. Wearing blue jeans and a white shirt, Barara walked unaided from the plane and disappeared into a white van with Taliban soldiers. He returned to the aircraft after ninety minutes.

Minutes after Barara was sent to the hospital, Burger lowered a short metal ladder from the cockpit. Carrying a pistol, he stood on the ladder for a few seconds, looked around at the airport building and then returned up the ladder. Everything seemed under control.

Hours crawled by.

Mumbai was waking up to another raucous day. The roads were already crowded in the Jogeshwari neighbourhood, cluttered by taxis, autorickshaws and directionless, uncontrolled crowds. Abdul Latif was up. A small crack team of the Crime Branch was alert, though they had spent a sleepless night. It was a tough vigil; they did not know what Latif's network was in the area, and how many people formed his Harkat-ul Mujahideen team in the metropolis. There was no word on whether they were armed. In the crowded neighbourhood, even the smallest suspicion could let their suspect get away, as well as endanger their own lives. The sharpshooters and other detectives were ready for a confrontation. All of them had revolvers concealed beneath their shirts. Latif stepped out of his house at about ten o'clock, looking confident as he walked out of the building in jeans and a T-shirt, with another man. They walked down the stairs and then hailed a passing autorickshaw. Both got in. Cars carrying the detectives tailed the autorickshaw, unnoticed. About one kilometre further, the other man got down and walked away. Latif was the one the detectives needed to concentrate on; the other man was ignored. About five hundred metres away, the autorickshaw was boxed in from several sides. Stunned and hopelessly outmanoeuvred, Latif gave up without a struggle. He then led the police to his flat in the Behrambagh area. Sharpshooters took position outside the door and barged in, expecting a gunbattle. But Latif's associate was too frightened and shocked to try to escape or put up resistance. They were arrested in the room with little else except a gray steel almirah and a bed — and two AK47 rifles, one anti-tank shell, six grenades, and a heap of Improvised Explosive Devices.

Within hours, more arrests were made as Latif started talking to his interrogators in a lockup where he was questioned by police and senior intelligence officials. Latif told the investigators about the hijacking plot, the preparation of several months, the hijackers' real names, several addresses of hijackers, the telephone numbers for some of them, and then directed the police to the people who had made their fake passports and driving licenses. Within a day, the police would have the hijackers' pictures as well.

Several layers of the hijacking mystery had been peeled off even before the hijacking ended.

Ibrahim Athar was speaking the truth when the aircraft set out from Lahore. He did have a millennium gift for India. Intelligence reports were making it clear that the hijackers had enough explosives to blow up the plane and a lot else, and they had planned that the plane would be blown up at midnight on 31 December. With the hijackers dangling their most serious threat so far over the lives of the passengers and some pressure from Mullah Omar, who wanted the negotiators to resume their discussions, the Indian side was back before the radio set in the control tower. This would be the decisive round of negotiations. The Taliban corps commander for Kandahar, Akhtar Mohammed Ismani, was also personally present in the control tower.

A Cabinet meeting in New Delhi a couple of hours ago had finally given the clearance for the deal, and Doval and Katju went into this round with a much more flexible mind than on previous days. Now they just had to minimise the damage. But Chief kept up a stern stance, refusing to agree to anything less than freedom for his elder brother and thirty-five other activists. He also threatened that if the talks broke down again, they would ask the pilot to take the plane to twenty thousand feet and blow it up. In the airport building, A.R. Ghanshyam, the Pakistan-based Indian diplomat who had arrived before the negotiators, described the hijackers as "intelligent and highly motivated people."

The Taliban leadership contributed to the drama and tension by ordering a fresh ring of turbaned commandos in shalwar kameezes, each carrying two AK47 machine guns, around the plane. A battle tank and rocket launchers were positioned near the aircraft, with the barrel towards the Indian relief plane. On another side, another truck carrying a US-made anti-aircraft Stinger missile was deployed near the aircraft. The Stingers had been brought to the airport to be sent to northern Afghanistan, to be used in the Taliban's battle with its enemies occupying ten per cent of the country's territory. Muttawakil then walked to the airport lounge where dozens of reporters were waiting for him, and announced that talks were now centred on the number of militants India would release. He clarified that the troops and the weaponry had been deployed "purely for security," and that the Taliban was not planning any operation.

Some time after the Taliban show of strength, the final deal was struck. The formula was to be worked out: the hijackers agreed to an arrangement that involved either the release of Masood Azhar and two others from a list to be given by Chief, or Masood and five others would be released from a list to be provided by the negotiators. Differences surfaced among the hijackers as well at this point over whose release should be demanded, presumably because at least two other hijackers — Doctor and Burger — also had their kin in Indian prisons. ATC officials in Kandahar heard shouts and loud arguments inside the cockpit, before Chief finally chose the first arrangement. He had the names ready: Apart from Maulana Masood Azhar, the Indian government would release militant leaders Ahmed Omar Syed Shaikh and Mushtaq Ahmed Zargar.

Few noticed that the three men were the same whose release had been demanded on the morning of 25 December, a day after the hijacking occurred, in the anonymous call to the New Delhi ATC. Six days and one killing later, the negotiators were signing the same deal.

Even before the final terms were decided, Burger walked out of the cockpit to the terrified passengers. They were waiting for their death sentence. He had a life-saving sentence instead: *"Tum sab ke liye achhi khabar hai.* Afghanistan *ki sarkar* third party *ban gayee hai aur unhone kaha hai ki vo kisi bekasoor* passenger *ko marne nahin denge"* (There is some good news for you. The Afghanistan government has agreed to act as a third party and they have said we will not let any innocent passenger die), he said. Burger praised Mullah Omar several times for "forcing" the Indian negotiators to agree to the deal.

An hour later, he brought the next instalment of the good news.

"Assi per cent *kaam ho gaya hai, bees* per cent *bacha hai. Dekha? Agar dil se dua karo to qubool ho jaati hai"* (Eighty per cent of the work is done. There is only twenty per cent left. See? If you pray from the depth of your heart your wishes come true), Burger said. *"Humne apne chhatees saathiyon ko*

[151]

chhorne ki baat kahi thi. Vo sirf teen par razi hue hain. Lekin hum aap begunah logon ko aur taqleef nahin dena chahte hain" (We had asked for the release of thirty-six of our comrades. They have agreed to release only three. But we do not want to let you innocent people suffer any longer), he beamed. Several passengers broke down, crying in relief. Some embraced their neighbours. The hijackers also embraced each other.

After about five minutes, Doctor emerged from the cockpit. He gave the thumbs-up sign. Chief stepped out a minute later, and shouted to his associates: *"Kaam ho gaya"* (The work is done). Burger shouted: *"Mubarakan!"* (Congratulations!) and then the five hijackers chorused an Islamic prayer. They said the agreement would take about ten to twelve hours to implement.

"Hum sab logon ko chhor denge. Sub final ho gaya hai. Hum dekh rahe hain kaise prisoners ko passengers mein badal dein" (We will release everyone. Everything has been finalised. We are working out how to change the prisoners into passengers).

It was past noon as a white UN plane touched down on the runway. It had brought 250 food packets, most of them vegetarian, prepared by the Pakistan International Airline's catering wing in Islamabad. It had also brought tubes of toothpaste and toothbrushes and the hostages brushed their teeth for the first time in a week. Waiting for them was their first sumptuous lunch since they left Kathmandu seven days ago.There were burgers, biscuits, fruits, milk, juice and soft drinks. Some diplomats had sent chocolates. It was as if a hundred celebrations had broken out at once. The hijackers asked the passengers to volunteer to serve the food, and to give the air hostesses a day off. Their lives intact, the hostages were only too happy to help.

Sanjive Sharma positioned himself near the open door — which was out of bounds for all for eight days — and picked up food packets from large bags to throw them to Ramesh Grover, who in turn passed them on ahead.

For many passengers, it would have seemed like tragic poetic justice: after seven days of living with Burger, they would get to eat one.

Burger told the passengers that their release had come mainly due to the efforts of the Amir of the Taliban — for whom he had great respect — and suggested that the passengers show their gratitude by giving him a gift. Money was pooled by the passengers, the foreign hostages paying in their own currencies, and Rs. 71,425 worth of cash was collected to buy a gift. One of the passengers was given part of the money to go to the Kandahar market to buy a gift, but he gave up the plan for fear of losing his relief plane. The amount was handed over to two Indian passengers, who were asked by Burger to buy a miniature areoplane and send it to the Amir through the Indian Embassy in Islamabad.

It was okay to laugh again. Nepali passenger Gajendra Man Tamrakar, earlier declared a hijacker by Indian officials by mistake, was sitting beside a Japanese woman. Burger had asked both of them to sit together because he said they looked similar. As the passengers started talking loudly about going home, Burger walked up to the Japanese woman and said, pointing to Tamrakar: "*Isse shaadi karogi?*" (Will you marry him?)

She paused for a second as she understood the question, blushed, and said: "No, I will marry you." Embarrassed, Burger walked away with a smile.

But Rajeev Ahuja, the man who always got into trouble with the hijackers and nearly got killed twice in the process, was not through with them yet. When he was pleading to be released along with other passengers in the UAE, Ahuja had told Burger that he had a serious heart ailment and doctors had predicted only about ten years of life for him.

Amid the celebration on board the plane, Ahuja forgot what he had told Burger and called out to an air hostess walking by: "Is there a beer can left?" Burger was sitting nearby. He suddenly turned to face Ahuja and said very sternly: "*Tu aur* beer? *Tune to kaha tha tere dil mein chhed hai? Tu* alcohol *kaise pee raha hai?*" (You having beer? I thought you had a hole in your heart! Why are you having alcohol?) Ahuja's hands turned cold. He smiled meekly and said: "*Maine socha mujhe dus barah saal main marna to hai hee, kyon na thoda aish kar lein*" (Well ... I thought since I have to die after 10-12 years... I might as well have some fun).

Burger was furious. He raised his revolver to Ahuja's head and thrust it against his temple. "*Dus barah saal mein marna hai to kyon na tere ko abhi maar doon?*" (Ten-twelve years? Then why don't I kill you now?). The other passengers also started shouting at Ahuja, saying he would get them into trouble after everything had been worked out.

Meanwhile, Doctor was about to start his second Islamic address of the week on the public address system. He spoke extempore — slowly and with conviction. It was hard to believe that the man speaking, as if from a pulpit, was the same man who had mercilessly ripped open a man's flesh and bled him to death.

"*Jaise bachche apne buzurgon ke saath bade hote hain, mazhab vo cheez hai jiske saath insaan bada hota hai. Jab aap Islam ke baare mein seekhte hain, aap achchaee aur buraee ke beech mein tameez karna seekh jate hain. Islam ka matlab hai sare mazhabon mein sabse pak*" (Religion is something a person learns as he grows up. When you learn about Islam, you learn to differentiate between evil and good. Islam means the purest of all religions)," he said.

"*Hum sochte hain hamein vo jawani mil sakti hai jis par budhape ka asar nahin parega, ya vo zindagi mil sakti hai jis par maut ka asar nahin hoga, ya vo amiri jis par garibi ka asar nahin hoga. Yeh sirf maut ke baad ho sakta hai*" (We believe we can get youth which will not be affected by old age, life which will not be affected by death, richness which will not be affected by misfortune. This happens only after death), Doctor's speech continued. "*Aapko Quran padhni chahiye, ye kaee jagah miltee hai*" (You should read the Koran, you can get it in various places).

Hundreds of other people were also resorting to religion, far away in New Delhi. Unaware that the ordeal of their kin was about to end, the relatives of the hostages assembled at the Indira Gandhi International Airport and set out together to worship different gods. They visited temples, churches, mosques and gurdwaras and prayed for the early release of the passengers.

Across the city at the Raj Ghat, the memorial of Mahatma Gandhi, hundreds of people prayed for the hostages. Some three hundred people belonging to eleven religions gathered by the black granite memorial. Saffron-robed Buddhist monks beat drums and knelt in prayer around the square memorial. They were joined by Hindus, Jews, Christians, Muslims and people from several other religions who sang religious hymns and chanted prayers for the safety of the passengers. Across the country, thousands of others were praying.

Despite the continuing agony of the relatives, the Indian government, unbelievably, would keep the information of the deal under wraps for one-and-a-half days, stretching the week-old trauma of the families — which was nearly life-threatening for some elderly relatives who could not bear the soaring tension and uncertainty. When journalists in New Delhi asked Foreign Minister Jaswant Singh and other officials about news agency reports from Kandahar related to the agreement between the negotiators and the hijackers, the officials flatly denied it.

Far away from Afghanistan's Kandahar city, crowds were growing at another Kandahar, the popular restaurant at a five star hotel in New Delhi, ahead of a party that was part of the millennium celebrations. In other swank party places across the city, hundreds of young people prepared to dance away into the night, the hungry, nearly-killed hostages of the plane in faraway Afghanistan seemed just a blur in time, just a story on the evening news bulletin. Tables were booked well in advance for millennium parties, shoppers were on a spree and business was booming. Nani Luthra, a twenty-year-old, shopping at Connaught Place, would sum up the feeling for the young party crowd: "Hey, these things happen. The concern is there but we do not connect on a personal level. All my friends are going to party."

Across the city at the international airport, one man who did know the agony of the people on Flight 814 was getting off a Pakistan International Airlines flight, which was ironically Flight 814 as well. Diabetic passenger Anil Khurana, freed by the hijackers on 26 December, was cheered by hundreds of people. Accompanied by his wife Neelu who had flown to Pakistan to be with her husband, Khurana was taken to a waiting ambulance immediately after the jetliner landed. Khurana greeted the people with a namaste before he was whisked away through the crowd of reporters and photographers.

A few hundred kilometres to the west, a police constable was furiously scribbling away on a large sheet of paper in a police station in Amritsar. A week after the hijacking of the aircraft, the police were making out a First Information Report against the hijackers for their crimes, including the killing of Ripan Katyal.

As evening fell over Jammu, a Research and Analysis Wing (RAW) jet descended over the airport carrying a top intelligence official who had gone to escort Maulana Masood Azhar from the Kot Bhalwal jail to New Delhi. But first, he had to get permission from Farooq Abdullah, chief minister of Jammu & Kashmir. This was a difficult decision for Abdullah, whose regime has witnessed a sharp rise in militant attacks after an initial slump. The release of three top honchos of terrorism in Kashmir was certain to send the morale of soldiers plummeting in a battle which is already sapping into the energies of battalions fighting insurgents rather than protecting the borders, because the state police has not been able to handle the problem on its own.

It would also be an embarrassing about-face for Abdullah, who had hours ago thundered against the release of the militants as he spoke to journalists after inaugurating an exhibition in Srinagar. Abdullah, who could have refused to release the militants, had said that the passengers should be released without making any compromise. "No militant should be released," he had told reporters. And yet, he was eating his words hours later, as the intelligence official persuaded him to order the release of the militants. Politics helped tilt the balance: Abdullah was an ally of Prime Minister Vajpayee's ruling coalition, his son was a minister in the Central government.

Of the three men being released, one — Maulana Masood Azhar — had never indulged in any terrorist activity himself; he just inspired people to take to terror. The other two were the men who, despite their diametrically opposite social backgrounds, rose to become the terror leaders of Kashmir.

Mushtaq Ahmed Zargar, thirty-three, better known as Mushtaq Latram, was born in Jammu & Kashmir. Latram had humble beginnings — he never made it past primary school and set up a shop to polish copper and brass utensils, but was soon introduced to crime. He started his career as a militant with the Jammu and Kashmir Liberation Front. According to a local legend, Zargar once led an attack on Indian soldiers in Srinagar with two assault rifles, one blazing from each hand. He was notorious for his barbaric ways, including tying hand grenades on the bodies of his victims and exploding them. Zargar became known in Srinagar by the nickname "Latram" which emerged from his frequent use of the words "Latram, Shatram" (talking nonsense). He founded a lean, ruthless outfit called the Al Umar and was one of the anchors of Kashmir's militant campaign when it broke out in 1989. He was arrested in 1992. Unlike Azhar, Zargar had little interest in religion. Also, unlike the Maulana who was disqualified from the armed training course in Afghanistan, Zargar revelled in violence and brutality and was described as a sadist. He was charged with responsibility for over three dozen murders in downtown Srinagar. He was the only resident of Kashmir on the list of thirty-six prisoners whose release the hijackers had sought.

Ahmed Omar Syed Shaikh, twenty-eight, would probably have been a Wall Street executive or a financial analyst had he not been swept into the insurgency. Shaikh was a

British national of Pakistani origin and held a post-graduate degree from the London School of Economics. He belonged to a rich family in Lahore, where he did his schooling before migrating to Britain. He joined the Harkat-ul Ansar outfit which was later declared a terrorist organisation by the US. He was arrested in 1994, and his name also appeared on the list of militants whose release was sought by the kidnappers of the five Western tourists in Kashmir in 1995. According to Indian officials, he had undergone special training in martial arts in Pakistan and Afghanistan. In October 1994, Shaikh was arrested from Ghaziabad town in Uttar Pradesh, hours after police rescued an American man who Shaikh had gagged, blindfolded and bound with a chain. Investigators later found that three other Britons, who were rescued, had also been abducted to force the release of Masood Azhar. Shaikh was lodged in New Delhi's Tihar Jail.

With such trails of crime behind him, the release of Zargar seemed a very brave decision for Farooq Abdullah, one that would ignore the concern of the security forces, as he sat in thought on the night of 30 December. It was midnight when Abdullah finally cleared the release. Masood Azhar was woken up and asked to pack. He would be released early on Friday.

At about 1:30 in the morning, officials stood outside the high security Srinagar prison, ready to take Zargar away. He was woken up and given time to pack his belongings, while the officials waited. At about 3:15 a.m., as thick fog made roads invisible in the chilly night, Zargar was driven out in a jeep with windows rolled up, travelling with another jeep in the front and one behind it. Several hours later, Zargar was sitting silently with two strangers in a helicopter as it droned high above cloud-kissed mountains.

*Astonishingly, when freedom comes, the hostages find it
difficult to say farewell to the hijackers ... they arrive
in Delhi amid scenes of joy and relief while in Kandahar,
the hijackers return to the aircraft at night ...*

Maulana Masood Azhar put on a washed, ironed
shalwar kameez, picked up his rosary and said a little
prayer. He had been woken up late the previous night by
prison officials and asked to pack his belongings. They did
not need to tell him why; the maulana had kept himself
updated on the hijacking crisis through the last week. Now,
it was about ten o'clock on 31 December. Though the
government had given no word yet about the release of the
three men, there were dozens of journalists waiting outside
the jail, a drill they had been following for several days now.
His armed guards in tow, Deputy Inspector-General of
Police S.P. Vaid drove into the Kot Bhalwal prison in
Jammu. He had been ordered to take Azhar to the technical

area of the Jammu airport, about twenty kilometres to the southwest of Jammu, from where VIP planes take off. Vaid looked at his watch and asked Jail Superintendent Chanchal Singh to get Azhar. Several minutes later, Azhar walked out of his cell and sauntered to where Vaid was standing. They looked each other in the eye.

"*Aap apna samaan le aaye hain?*" (Have you got your baggage?), Vaid asked.

"*Ji*" (Yes), Azhar replied, and showed his bag. He smiled.

"*Hamen aapka chehra dhakna parega. Aisa karne se apko saans lene me taqlif to na hogi?*" (We will have to cover your face. Will you have difficulty breathing?), Vaid asked courteously. He was actually thinking about the crowd of journalists outside. The maulana would have to be taken undetected.

"*Aap beshak mera chehra dhak len per meri ankhen khuli rahne den*" (Go ahead and cover my face but leave my eyes open), Azhar said. Vaid asked him why.

"*Maine Quran Sharif parhni hai. Ajkal Ramzan ka mahina hai*" (I have to read the Quran Sharif. These are the days of Ramzan), he said. The officer was getting edgy. This polite conversation could delay the flight to New Delhi that Azhar was to take.

Vaid snapped: "*Aap Quran zarur parhiye magar ankh khulne ke bad. Tab tak aap khuda ko bina Quran parhe bhi yaad kar sakte hain. Andhe bhi to khuda ko yaad karte hain*" (Sure, read the Quran but after your eyes are opened. Until then, you can remember God even without reading the Quran. After all, blind people also pray). Azhar did not reply. A constable opened the doors of a white Maruti Gypsy car and Azhar stepped inside. He was blindfolded. There was one escort car in front of the Maruti, one behind. Vaid took his front seat and asked the driver to go to the airport. They sat in the Gypsy for thirty-five minutes without saying a word. The three cars raced to the Jammu airport. Zargar had arrived.

In the Cabinet Room in the prime minister's South Block office in New Delhi, Foreign Minister Jaswant Singh was making an unexpected proposal at the meeting of the Cabinet Committee on Security. He volunteered to go to Kandahar with the three prisoners, ostensibly to try and convert the week-long communication with the Taliban, formerly adversaries, into a more firm relationship. The other ministers hesitated, some objected, but the Cabinet finally gave its assent. However, sharp differences had already emerged within the government over the handling of the crisis, and the final deal. The most outspoken critic was Home Minister Lal Krishna Advani, who would voice his criticism publicly. Defence Minister George Fernandes also was unhappy with the way the compromise was reached.

Jaswant Singh emerged from the meeting and announced he would fly to Kandahar to try and end the crisis. But the impatient crowds of journalists would know only later in the day that Singh would have three co-passengers as well in the Boeing 737. The aircraft was ready at the airport, but the three men were yet to arrive. The flight from Jammu was delayed due to bad weather.

Yes, there were warm thoughts of homecoming, but it had still been a freezing night. The hostages in Kandahar had barely slept the whole night, but for the first time in a week this was out of hope, not despair — they were waiting to go home. There had also been no sleep because the auxilliary power unit had shut down again at about 3:30 in the morning, plunging the plane once again into darkness. To avoid the stench from the toilets, the doors were opened once again, suddenly exposing the passengers to the sub-zero temperatures outside. There were no blankets for most passengers. They wore their socks, draped jackets and shawls around themselves, and put their feet up on their seats close to their bodies to try and keep warm.

It was morning now; the hijackers asked the passengers to slide open the window shutters. To the outsiders, even this small activity appeared like magic in the aircraft that had stood silent like a mountain for seven days on the tarmac. Beginning from the back rows, one by one the windows went up as if run by a mechanism. The bright sunlight filtered in. Chilly gusts of wind also swept in through the open doors. The fear of death no longer gnawing into them, passengers peered out of their windows like spellbound tourists. It was a beautiful morning: the mountaintops appeared hazy in the distance, lost in furrows of clouds; on another side, part of Kandahar city could be seen, with the glittering white dome of a mosque looming above the patchwork of houses. Then they looked down, on the tarmac below them, and there was a small group of Taliban soldiers, in green shalwar kameez puffed up by the wind, who were down on their knees on the bare tarmac, two machine guns kept on the ground by the side of each soldier. Their foreheads touched the tarmac. It was time for namaz, and some passengers sitting close to the doors heard the faint call of the muezzin echo across the city from the mosque.

A white bus raced on the bleak, desolate tarmac, the airport almost totally silent, and was parked about ten metres away from the plane, facing the cockpit. Preparations were beginning for the release of passengers later in the day. It was a very cold day. Taliban men walked about with their bodies wrapped in shawls right up to their heads. Then two engineers started work on the auxilliary power unit. Four men in shawls pushed a huge blue iron ladder mounted on a trolley with wheels that creaked loudly. All four men leaned hard against it as they pushed the trolley to below the tail of the aircraft. One engineer climbed up and his torso disappeared inside the metallic hulk, the legs still visible on the ladder.

Outside the airport building, a white van resembling an ambulance with a yellow blinking light on top screeched to a halt near gun-toting soldiers. The bearded Afghan driver wearing a white Muslim cap hopped out and opened the doors for the occupants to step out. One by one, Indian officials stepped out, looking tired and deprived of sleep. But relief was apparent on their faces — like the hostages and the hijackers and the diplomats, they were also getting to go home. Waiting cameramen zoomed in. One Sikh official laughed and said: "Let me do my hair first!"

In the distance in the airport lounge, diplomats from different countries stood talking. Hours passed by.

In the plane, passengers heard a faint drone in the distance. It soon became louder and a UN plane appeared on the horizon. Lunch had arrived. Soon another UN plane landed. Burger was pacing in the aisle, as restless as the others to get out of the plane. "*Hamare bhai aa gaye*" (Our brothers have come), he muttered as he walked. Passenger Vishal Sharma, sitting next to where he stood, said: "UN planes." Burger turned back and said : "*Vah, badi tez nigah hai bhai*" (Wow, sharp eyes, you noticed quickly).

"*Subah se runway se aankh hataee nahin hai*" (I haven't taken my eyes off the runway since morning), Sharma said still staring at the runway. About thirty minutes later, an

Afghan military jet, painted in green, landed on the same runway.

Shankar got down from the aircraft to supervise the arrangements. He moved unrestricted around the area, looking in control. Shankar spoke to an Indian official standing nearby, then gestured as he talked to a Taliban soldier who held a radio set, walked around the aircraft for about fifteen minutes and then went to sit inside a dark blue Pajero. He walked confidently, his hands dug deep into the pockets of a large jacket in blue and black colours, wearing a pair of black jeans, and a red monkey cap.

The activity at the airport suddenly seemed to be increasing. Four Taliban commandos in green army fatigues, machine guns slung on both shoulders and their turban ends billowing in the air, stood on an open Toyota pick-up van as it raced right up to the plane and stopped near the Pajero. One of the commandos jumped off and walked to the car, where he talked to Shankar through the window. After about thirty minutes, a bulky Taliban official walked up to the Pajero, peeped inside and ushered Shankar outside as he gestured with his hand. He walked inside the plane. Members of the Indian team, apparently engineers, stood waiting near the airport building carrying large cubical iron boxes painted in green, red, blue and black, and a large yellow torch. Soon after, a step ladder was brought to the aircraft and the men with boxes climbed up and into the plane.

In the airport building, Katju walked with a red muffler thrown around his neck and furrows on his forehead. Some distance away, an Indian official furiously took notes as he spoke on a satellite phone with New Delhi. With help from the Taliban, the hijackers had done a little turnaround overnight over the exact manner of the exchange. It was earlier agreed that the hijackers would remain inside the aircraft while the passengers walked out, and then the five men would leave. Overnight, the hijackers changed their minds about the way the exchange would take place. The new plan was: the three prisoners would be released from the aircraft carrying Jaswant Singh; they would be driven up to the hijacked aircraft where the hijackers would identify them; then the hijackers would leave with the three men, followed by the hostages. Indian officials protested, but the Taliban stood firm on the new plan and backed the hijackers.

Taliban Foreign Minister Muttawakil had already dashed the negotiators' hopes that his government would take the hijackers into custody and try them according to Taliban law — this would have meant a sentence of capital punishment. Mullah Omar and other Taliban officials had repeatedly declared the hijacking illegal and Muttawakil also said that they did not support the hijackers despite their being Muslims. But Muttawakil did another turn-around Friday morning, and told the Indian officials that the hijackers would not be arrested, rather they would be given ten hours to leave Afghanistan. Both the hijackers and the hostages were to leave like guests leave.

Jaswant Singh, the man who was bringing the three tickets to the hostages' freedom, was boarding the Alliance Air Boeing 737 in New Delhi. The flight had been delayed by several hours because of the delay in the arrival of the Jammu flight. Accompanied by a senior official of his ministry, Singh was still on the phone, speaking with the negotiators in Kandahar. He walked to the business class. A few minutes later, top officials of the home ministry and security guards escorted his unlikely co-travellers —

Maulana Masood Azhar, Mushtaq Ahmad Zargar and Ahmed Omar Syed Shaikh. They were seated in the rear of the plane.

State Minister for External Affairs Ajit Panja and Foreign Secretary Lalit Mansingh, meanwhile, were meeting ambassadors of different countries whose hostages were on the plane, and informing them of the government's decision. Outside the government, among the first to know were the ambassadors of Japan, Spain and France; the high commissioners of Canada and Australia, and the charge d'affaires of Belgium.

One block away, at the prime minister's office, National Security Adviser Brajesh Mishra emerged from another tense meeting and finally made the deal with the hijackers public. Mishra also said that the hijackers would be dealt with according to the law of the Taliban. Since the Taliban had already decided that it would not arrest the hijackers, it is not known whether this was a fond hope or repetition of a promise made by the Taliban that it went back on.

In Kandahar, a little skit was being staged inside the plane — and Gajendra Man Tamrakar of Nepal, who, ironically, had repeatedly been labelled a hijacker, was about to get the distinction of being the last man to be whacked by the hostage-takers. As the passengers waited for the relief plane to arrive from New Delhi, Tamrakar was asked to perform a scene from the hugely popular film *Sholay*, one of the hundreds of Hindi films made in India which have a mass following in Nepal.

"*Tum mujhe maaroge*" (You will beat me), he said. Burger promised no one would beat him, and asked him to perform whatever he wanted as he handed the small-time Nepali stand-up comedian a hand-held microphone. As the passengers broke into loud giggles, Tamrakar cleared his throat and began enacting a hugely popular scene that has become part of Indian cultural folklore — when the bandit Gabbar Singh punishes his three henchmen for failing to capture the two protagonists who wanted to bust the bandits' gang.

"Kitne aadmi the?" (How many men were they?)

"Sarkaar, paanch" (Master, five), Tamrakar said, referring to the hijackers.

"Vo paanch, aur tum ek sau saath, phir bhi bach gaye? Bahut nainsafee hai, bahut nainsafee hai" (They were ive, and you 160, still they got away? This is too bad, too bad). This was probably the bravest statement a hostage had made — and gotten away with — and Tamrakar got bolder.

"Tera kya hoga, Kalia?" (What about you, Blackie?), Tamrakar said, looking at Burger, who was dressed in a black T-shirt and a pair of black jeans. Burger smiled and folded his hands, pretending to be scared, and bowed his head.

"Sarkar, maine pichhle aath din se aapka namak khaya hai" (Master, I have been loyal to you for the last eight days), Tamrakar spoke on behalf of Burger as he copied dialogues from the movie with a mischievous twist.

The passengers burst out laughing. So Tamrakar did the unimaginable — he mimicked the jumpy and aggressive Bhola, using the sentences he had often used as he enforced discipline among the hostages. Bhola stood nearby.

"Neeche dekhen sab! Chup kar baith jao! Mama ki shaadi mein aae ho?" (Look down! Don't make a noise! Have you come to your uncle's wedding?) Bhola got furious and took a wild swing, hitting Tamrakar on the head with the revolver butt. He returned sulking to his seat with a

swelling on his forehead. But Tamrakar would say later: "It was the greatest show I ever put up."

In the skies overhead, Capt. R.N. Singh was beginning the descent of the Alliance Air Boeing towards the Kandahar airport. Jaswant Singh had finally arrived with the three released prisoners. The plane touched down; ground control asked it to park in a bay about half a mile from where the hijacked aircraft was. It raced past barbed fences, a yellow bulldozer and dozens of rusting iron girders strewn by the runway and came to a halt.

Four empty buses were driven up to the tarmac near the hijacked Airbus 300. Several wheelchairs and boxes of water bottles were also carted close. About thirty Taliban soldiers took up positions, holding automatic rifles. Others sat cross-legged along the runway. Near the airport lounge, Taliban officials were cautioning journalists not to be over-enthusiastic when the exchange took place, as it was not known how the hijackers might react. "Whatever happens, don't rush toward the plane, it could be dangerous," Muttawakil warned. "The whole hijacking is a very dangerous business."

The hostages started to prepare themselves for freedom. Astonishingly, farewell seemed difficult. Many passengers would miss the five men who had turned their lives upside down, thrashed them, threatened to kill them, deprived them of food and water and confined them forcibly to a place that became something of a pigsty. Many passengers would see Burger and Doctor and the rest in their dreams. Some women would even fantasise about them. It was the most puzzling, most mystifying of human emotions — several people were actually feeling bad because the people who hurt them were going. As passenger Satish Sahni would say weeks after the hijacking: "I would certainly love to shake hands once again with a man like Burger."

Burger spent the last one hour chatting. *"Main bahut khush hoon ki aap sab log ghar ja rahe hain"* (I am very happy that all of you are going home), he said. He had brought a Christmas card with a little message on its back that an anxious mother had written for her little daughter. She had handed it to him so that he could somehow have it sent to her daughter if she died on the plane. Burger returned the card to the woman.

Burger added another uncharacteristic apology: *"Jo hua uske liye humein maaf kar dena. Ye hamare bus ke bahar tha"* (Forgive us for what has happened. It was beyond our control). It was nearly three o'clock.

All ready to leave, Chief walked up to Jaggia and said: *"Hamara kaam ho gaya hai. Hamara* baggage *de deejiye. Koi nuksaan ho gaya to hamaree zimmedaari nahin hogi"* (Our work is done. Please give us our baggage. If there is any damage, we will not be responsible). But it was not realised until, after the hijackers left, that he was talking about a bag in the baggage hold.

He had checked in this bag weighing seventeen kilograms containing RDX at the Kathmandu airport, wired to explode at midnight on 31 December. It is not known if all of it was RDX, but one would need only one kilogram of the explosive to blow up the plane. RDX is light yellowish in colour like plasticene and resembles bad smelling dough. It is a lethal explosive with tremendous impact, is light in weight and cannot be traced by a metal detector, which makes it most useful for terrorists. Its explosion has a shattering impact that travels at about sixty thousand to eighty-five thousand feet per second. Within a fraction of a second, the aircraft could become pulp.

[170]

Half a mile away, Jaswant Singh stepped out of the Alliance Air plane. An impressive motorcade was waiting for him. As he stepped into a black Mercedes, the motorcade started moving slowly, two immaculately dressed Afghans wearing black uniforms and white helmets leading the way on BMW motorcycles. They were followed by a silver Toyota car, followed by a Russian-made Volga car with red stripes and a flashing red light on top, a white Toyota, a dark blue Pajero, a brown four-wheel drive Landrover, a black Mercedes and another white Toyota. Loud sirens heralded the arrival of the Indian foreign minister. Singh was driven away to meet Muttawakil and the diplomats.

Then Masood, Zargar and Shaikh were led out of the plane and escorted to the waiting Pajero. The car drove right up to the hijacked aircraft. A metallic ladder was lowered from the cockpit and Burger came out. Chief came out next, and Burger held the ladder so that it might not shake. Chief was immediately escorted by a Taliban commander and both walked along the plane as they spoke. Now was the moment he had staked the lives of the passengers for: before him, much more plump than when they last met, was his elder brother, Maulana Masood Azhar, free from jail. The maulana stepped forward, and as he did, used his strong elbow to push aside an Indian official who was standing in the way. They embraced each other tightly for several minutes, and then Chief huddled with Taliban corps commander Usmani to discuss something. Burger went up again into the aircraft, to say his goodbyes to the passengers. He embraced about twenty people one by one, tears in his eyes, and waved wildly at everyone. Flight Engineer Jaggia had a gift for Burger. He called him as the hijackers were about to leave.

"*Aap ko main jab bhi dekhta hoon, mujhe apne abba ki yaad aati hai*" (Whenever I see you, I remember my father), Burger told Jaggia.

"I will give you a gift," Jaggia said, as he thrust his big red torch into Burger's hands. "*Tum ek achche insaan ho. Tumhe sahi rasta dekhne ke liye ye chahiye*" (You are a good human being. You need this to see your path).

"Bye, *Allah ne chaha to phir milenge*. We love you all!" (God willing we shall meet again), Burger shouted as he walked back towards the cockpit. "*Agar humne koi galti ki ho ya aap logon ko nahak pareshan kiya ho to hamein maaf kar dein*" (If we have have done any mistake, or if we have unnecessarily harassed anybody, we are sorry). Then he embraced passenger Sanjive Sharma and wept on his shoulder, tears streaming out of his mask.

One by one, the four remaining hijackers, all still masked, came down from the aircraft using the same cockpit ladder. Burger remained in the cockpit until he threw down each bag through the opening to Bhola, who caught them below and kept them on the tarmac. Burger got down last, leaping in mid-air half-way down the ladder. A Taliban soldier picked up the bags, one by one, and kept them in the waiting Land Rover. Some more drama remained. Corps Commander Usmani's brother, a bulky, turbaned man in shalwar kurta, was about to say something to Shankar when he took out his revolver and held it towards him, gesturing with his hand that he should raise his hands and not try to come close. He was thoroughly frisked. Behind him, Bhola also stood holding a revolver. The junior Usmani was to be a hostage for the hijackers, ostensibly until they crossed Afghanistan's territory. All the bags stashed in the vehicle, the four hijackers joined Chief who was already seated inside. The three released prisoners were in a second car, both parked on the side of the hijacked aircraft. Two other Pajeros were escorting these two vehicles. Then a Taliban official jogged towards the car, waved his hands and asked them to leave. With the hijackers waving pistols in the air from the windows, the four vehicles raced away, taking a semi-circle before speeding away on a road leading out of the airport. The hijackers' car was leading the little caravan. A crimson sun was about to slide down the horizon behind the dark profile of the aircraft they had controlled for eight days. The longest-running hijacking drama in a decade had come to an end. It was the last sunset of the millennium.

The four buses slowly moved towards the aircraft. A passenger step ladder was driven to the plane. A tank and a truck with a Stinger missile mounted on it stood some distance away. Inside, Capt. Sharan was asking passengers to make sure they had all the luggage they brought, not a single item more. The crew was conscious of the "millennium gift" that Ibrahim Athar had left in the plane. As the hijackers disappeared into the horizon, a team of Indian doctors waiting several hundred yards away from the aircraft rushed towards it. They rushed up the ladders, expecting emergencies, but only seven people needed slight treatment. The thought of a homecoming had healed the rest of all ailments. The passengers were ready with their baggage and the crew had conducted a thorough search of the aircraft. The hijackers had left behind nothing apart from their night vision binoculars.

First, the men came out. Then the women, with their faces under anything that resembled a veil, in accordance with Taliban regulations. The women covered their faces in saris and dupattas, draping them around their foreheads and mouths, with only the eyes visible. Taliban soldiers scrutinised the baggage as the weary passengers got out of the aircraft to board another one. The hijacked plane would follow them after repairs. The passengers stepped down, and suddenly the airport that had an eerie calm for seven days broke into chaos. Though there were two relief planes standing, officials were unsure of how exactly the transfer would take place. Some officials carrying lists of passengers tried to tally their names, but this angered the passengers desperate to reach home as soon as possible. Then an official suggested that men and women come in separate aircraft — and the husbands and wives nearly threatened not to board the plane. After the hijackers' terror, Indian bureaucracy had taken over.

Singh now faced the extremely difficult task of defending the humiliating deal at a press conference; he also had to defend the Taliban action of letting the hijackers go honourably insead of arresting and trying them. As he stood with Taliban Foreign Minister Muttawakil, who stood expressionless with not a hint of a smile on his face, Singh said:

"We had stated at the very beginning that our main concern was the termination of the hijacking and the safe return of all the hostages and crew. I wish to place on record my sense of gratitude and indebtedness to the support and cooperation that we have received from the Taliban and also from his Excellency personally. India's fight against such criminal acts ... shall continue. I also wish to say that according to what has been informed by his Excellency, they shall not receive any asylum in Afghanistan. They have ten hours within which they can go wherever they wish to go."

As he turned to go, he replied to the only and obvious question: "There is no bowing down to terrorism now, or ever again."

The plane had to take off at the earliest because the Kandahar airport was not Y2K compliant, and it had no facilities for night take-off. Singh was then taken by Muttawakil to a waiting vehicle before he got into the relief aircraft, to end the first ever visit by any Indian government minister during the Taliban regime. It was a peculiar sight: Muttawakil, his eyelids half-closed and his face sombre, walked ahead as he held Singh's right hand and pulled him along, ushering him out of his country. When they stood before the waiting car, Singh extended his hand for a handshake. Muttawakil turned away and gestured for him to sit in the car.

As the passengers entered the relief aircraft, pent-up emotions erupted; the air hostesses of the relief plane hugged the women one by one, congratulated them and wept loudly. Then nearly all the passengers, with uncontrollable kidneys and bowels, lined up outside the toilets. They were going to see a luxury after eight days: a clean toilet.

In India, Prime Minister Vajpayee was beginning his nationally televised speech on the state-run Doordarshan channel, trying to make the best out of an embarrassing defeat in a battle against five desperate men, one of them a murderer. Vajpayee had earlier planned to be at the airport with several Cabinet members to receive the passengers when they arrived, but the plan was cancelled due to security risks. He said:

"A new chapter in the history of mankind begins as the sun sets for the last time in the twentieth century.

"This is an occasion for cheer and joy.

"Doubly so because the ordeal of our sisters and brothers, of the little children, held hostage by the hijackers of an Indian Airlines plane is nearing an end. They will soon be back with their families to usher in the New Year. As you are aware, the government was guided by two concerns: the safety of the passengers and the crew, and the long-term, overall interests of our country.

"The hijacking of the Indian Airlines plane once again reminds us of the terrible reality of terrorism. The hijacking, diabolic and evil as it is, is but the latest manifestation. We must not spare any effort, India shall not spare any effort to thwart the phenomenon itself."

A few hours after they vanished into the desert expanse, the four vehicles carrying the hijackers, the released prisoners and Taliban security guards did a U-turn on the road leading up to Pakistan. They returned to Kandahar. The Indian relief planes carrying the hostages and government officials had taken off several hours ago. Now only the hijacked plane remained. The dark blue Pajero in which the hijackers had stuffed their lugagge and then driven away, was back. It roared into the airport in the dark, its headlights lighting up part of the runway from far away as it approached the plane.

Ibrahim Athar had mysteriously changed his mind within a few hours.

He did not want to give the "millennium gift" he had left for India in the luggage hold of the hijacked plane. He wanted it back. Athar had earlier planned a sensational end to the hijacking drama, identical to a 29-year-old hijacking. On 30 January 1971, Hashim and Ashraf Quereshi, brothers and members of the Jammu and Kashmir Liberation Front, hijacked Ganga, a Fokker Friendship aircraft of the Indian

Airlines flying from Srinagar to Jammu. Armed with a pistol and a hand grenade, they then forced the pilot to fly to Lahore — considered the most hijacking-friendly destination for Indian flights. Prime Minister Yahya Khan's foreign minister, Zulfiqar Ali Bhutto, rushed to Lahore after the aircraft had landed. On 1 February, Bhutto persuaded the hijackers to release the crew and passengers who returned to India through the road route, crossing the border at the main check post of Wagah in Punjab. The hijackers were not arrested. India's government requested Pakistani authorities to permit them to send a replacement crew to fly back the hijacked aircraft. But a day after the hostages were released, the hijackers mysteriously came to possess powerful explosives, of which they had made no mention earlier. They blew up the aircraft.

Ibrahim Athar had agreed to the release of passengers. Now he had to blow up the aircraft. But he decided against it, possibly to avoid putting the Taliban, which had been good friends during the crisis, into an embarrassing situation even before the teams from international media organisations left town.

It was about 11 p.m. The Pajero drove right up to the aircraft, its bright headlights the only source of light apart from the aircraft's lights. No one got down. It is not known how many people were inside; but the occupants certainly included at least one hijacker. Taliban soldiers on guard nearby climbed up and into the plane. They told the Indian crew members to leave the aircraft. Then a makeshift step ladder tall enough to reach the baggage hold was wheeled to the aircraft, and the Taliban soldiers opened the luggage hold. They knew exactly what to look for and where. The Taliban soldier on top of the ladder took out a reddish golf bag and held it up as it shone in the headlights. It was the bag they were looking for, and the soldier climbed down. He passed it inside the car.

The Pajero melted away in the darkness. Its next destination, and the final one for the night, was a guest house not far from the airport. It was the same guest house where the Indian negotiators had been staying so far and where several Western diplomats were staying even now, as the hijackers walked in. As a diplomat would describe later, they were given a room which was vacated a few hours ago — the same one where some members of the Indian team had stayed.

As Amit Jain emerged from the aircraft, it seemed as if he had been thrown into a sea of people. It was 8:47 in the evening. The first of the two relief aircraft had landed, and there were thousands of relatives, friends, airport employees, bystanders, police and journalists cheering lustily as the pale and tired passengers started to step down. The crowd in front of Jain was surging and jostling every minute. It was a noisy homecoming. About thirty minutes later, the second flight landed.

"*Bharat Mata ki Jai!*" Patriotic slogans echoed through across the tarmac. The passengers and the onlookers raised their fists in the air. Cameras clicked and zoomed furiously. Journalists fought with police. Huge bouquets of flowers bobbed in the crowds. Some trembling, others waving, many weeping, the passengers got down slowly from the step ladder and were swept into the carnival of ecstatic relatives. A thousand embraces followed. An elderly woman hugged her son until she fainted. The relatives hoisted their kin on their shoulders or tossed them into the air. They screamed at journalists trying to ask the exhausted passengers endless questions. Many passengers were taken in ambulances to hospitals, but most wanted to just go home, and were whisked away through the throngs. Few were able or willing to speak. A column of ambulances and police vehicles waited to rush the former hostages to hospitals or their homes. Foreign hostages were taken to their embassies.

Nearly two hundred hours after they took off from Kathmandu, the hostages had reached New Delhi. In three hours, it would be a new millennium. It was already a new life.

As the Indira Gandhi International Airport erupted into an extended celebration, one car was already racing down a highway dimly lit by looming street lights. Twenty-eight days after her wedding, Rachna Katyal, wife of Ripan Katyal, was returning from her honeymoon. Alone. She had emerged from the aircraft dizzy and stunned, with two ladies holding her, and now she was on her way home — unaware, even now, that her husband had been brutally killed by the hijackers eight days ago. "*Aap log mujhe Ripan ke paas kyon nahin le chalte? Meri kasam khao ki vo theek hain*" (Why don't you take me to Ripan? Swear on me that he is fine), she repeatedly asked her relatives at the airport. An hour later, she was back at her Sector 14 residence in Gurgaon, a dark blob amid an ocean of glittering lights as the rest of the town readied itself for the new millennium. A group of men dressed in white had walked into the house a few hours ago after the kriya ceremony held for Ripan at the local Community Centre. Now she walked in, looked for her husband, and did not find him there. An hour later, a few minutes after midnight as the town was engulfed in a raucous celebration, her weeping relatives told Rachna what everybody else had known all this while. Stunned and disbelieving, she wept and howled into the night on her bed until she had to be put to sleep with tranquilisers. Even as she became drowsy, she cried out, *"Mujhe Ripan ke paas le chalo! Mujhe Ripan ke paas le chalo! Unhone use maar diya!"* (Take me to Ripan! They have killed him!).

THE DAYS AFTER

*The hijackers sleep in the same guest house where
Indian negotiators had stayed, and later find safe haven in
Pakistan ... Maulana Masood Azhar makes incendiary
speeches ... and Rachna Katyal cries out in her sleep*

The long telephone ring echoed in the house in
Bahawalpur, the small town in eastern Pakistan. It was
almost dark. Former school teacher Allah Baksh Sabir
walked to the phone; it was a call he had been waiting for
the whole day. His son, Maulana Masood Azhar, was speaking on a satellite phone a few hours after being freed. He
said he was in Kandahar and would be home in a few days.
As one of the daughters of Allah Baksh watched silently,
father and son were engrossed for a long time in a deep
discussion. Days before Eid, the flourishing family of Allah
Baksh was about to come together in a huge homecoming.

It was a lonely house. The old man was father of a dozen
children — six sons and six daughters. But four of his sons
were away. Masood was in jail, Abdul Rauf Asgar was
away in Karachi, Ibrahim Athar was on his mission. (Allah

Baksh would tell the world that Athar was on a pilgrimage).
Young Jehangir Akbar was in a madrassa in a small town
near Bahawalpur. That left another son, Mohammad Tahir
Anwar, as the man of the house, the man who would take
care of everything at the poultry and dairy farm that Allah
Baksh owned, who would answer the hundreds of phone
calls about his brother's release with a gentle "*Salaam
A'laikum*" — and the youngest son, Mohiuddin Alamgir,
now in the ninth grade. Of the daughters, four were married, leaving only Safia Bibi and Sumeera Bibi. It wasn't
such a crowded house, but it would soon be: his sons were
coming back, and there was going to be a wedding. Allah
Baksh had decided that he was going to have Masood
Azhar married off.

In Kandahar, the dark blue Pajero in which the maulana
was travelling had returned late on 31 December. The eight
men — five hijackers and the three prisoners — saw no
reason in travelling across the border right away. It was
getting dark. From the Kandahar airport, the nearest border
crossing into Pakistan at Chaman was three to four hours
away to the southeast in mountainous territory. The route
to the expansive, porous border in the remote mountain
desert region was taken all the time by drug traffickers and
other smugglers. It would take almost four more hours for
them to drive from Chaman past Pishin and Bostan towns
to reach the nearest big town, Quetta — also a major military base in the North-west Frontier Province. But it would
be nearly two in the morning by the time they reached
there. Wiser counsel prevailed; the Taliban hosts had warm
beds ready, and the group stayed back at the guest house.
There was very little to fear; Muttawakil had already made
it clear to the world media that the Taliban was not going
to give away the whereabouts of the hijackers.

What happened over the next few days is not clear. According to conversations between members of the Harkat-ul Mujahideen that investigators listened into, the group crossed the mountainous Khojak Pass near Chaman sometime during the day, and went up to the town of Gulistan, but turned back for some reason. It is possible they wanted to avoid the main route of Chaman, because dozens of journalists were still driving back into Pakistan through that route after covering the hostage crisis. Pakistani officials said that the country was on "high alert" to prevent the hijackers from crossing the 1,000-mile (1,600 kilometres) border, which has many mountain passes that are the favourite routes of smugglers into Pakistan. But several journalists who took the route said only two unarmed guards were on duty at the Chaman post and there was no sign of high security. The easiest way to walk undetected across the frontier was to walk a short distance away from the border post and cross into Pakistan.

By Monday, the family of Allah Baksh was getting worried. As one of the daughters would tell a journalist who called that day, Maulana Masood Azhar and his younger brother had not arrived. They hadn't even called since the Friday evening conversation. Azhar finally returned to Bahawalpur on Friday, 7 January, a whole week after the hijacking ended — without his younger brother. About two hundred relatives, friends and neighbours thronged his house and welcomed him with reverence. On the tenth — a day after Eid — he got married to a girl who teaches in a local religious school. It was a simple marriage ceremony at a mosque in Bahawalpur; only twelve relatives were present. It seemed as if the maulana had got himself released only to wear a wedding sehra, but the wedding was only to keep his parents happy: he told his wife immediately after the wedding that he would endure a six-month separation from her to devote time to recruiting fighters for Kashmir.

Hundreds of kilometres away in a sleepy neighbourhood in Srinagar near one of the gates of the Jama Masjid, one woman had had a sehra for her son in her mind for a long time. The skinny woman with sunken cheeks, with her hands bare except for two gold bangles, sat silently in front of the huge portrait of a young man with a careless smile. It was Tuesday, 3 January. This was the three-storeyed house of Mushtaq Ahmad Zargar, or Mushtaq Latram, the terror of Srinagar who had been released from a prison cell. Salima, the skinny woman, was Zargar's mother. She had given birth to him in this house. Now he was free but instead of celebrating his freedom, she feared for his life. She had cried several times since she heard of her son's release. He was without the safety of the solid iron bars now, he was in the open; it was a jungle out there.

Latram's sister was busy attending to dozens of guests who were streaming in to congratulate the mother in an unending stream. The phone rang. It was him. He said he was calling from Muzaffarabad in Pakistan-controlled Kashmir. Outside the house, people spoke of Latram in hushed voices laced with fear and reverence. It seemed the old days were back again.

Until then, in Lahore, Ahmed Umar Saeed Shaikh had not reached home or called his father Ahmed Saeed Shaikh, the wealthy owner of a flour mill in Lahore, capital of the Punjab state.

In India, there were already strong rumours that apart from releasing the three prisoners, the government had also paid two hundred million US dollars to the hijackers. One of the hostages who has close links with a top aide of the prime minister also said he knew that the ransom had been paid. But it was not possible to get more information on these rumours. Parliamentary Affairs Minister Pramod Mahajan had denied them on 31 December: "Nobody is happy to release any terrorist, but it was a bargain against the lives of 155 hostages. No money has been given to the hijackers and there is nothing beyond the deal to release three terrorists."

On 4 January, two Harkat-ul Mujahideen activists in Pakistan sounded worried about a "consignment" that came after the hijackers and had not reached its destination. Indian intelligence officials say the two men who addressed each other as Irfan and Jajje could be speaking of money or arms in this intercepted conversation, but this could well be only intelligent guesswork. The conversation mentions Mansoor — Mohammad Mansoor is the real name of Burger or Sunny Ahmed Qazi, and also refers to one of the released militants as Afjosh, as having reached Karachi.

Irfaan: Hello...

Jajje: Haan, Irfan? (Yes, Irfaan?)

Irfan: Haan, Jajje ki hal hai? (Jajje, how are you?)

Jajje: Tera phone *nee aanda bachche?* (Why didn't you call me, kid?)

Irfaan: Vo Jajje aisa hai ki vo Kandaharon maal utho nikla hai, vo mainu roz phone karda to mainu batawe, tafseel bhool janda ki kedi kitti kitti tafseel hai. (Jajje, it's like this; The consignment has left Kandahar for that side. He calls me everyday and tells me, but I am forgetting the details.)

Jajje: Kandahar chho banda pahunchda hai do ghainte lagdene, maal pahunchne main kinne panja din lagdene... (It takes two hours for a man to reach Kandahar. Will it take five days for the consignment to reach?)

Irfaan: Utthe Taliban di ghumraich time lagge na, chaar din ho gaye maal nikla hai, vo Hila tak pahuncha hi nahin haiga, hun tak Chaman *main hai. Hun gal karke rakha hai, kainde hain Hila tak naee pahuncha.* (I hope the Taliban doesn't delay it. It's been four days now and the consignment has not reached Hila, it is still at Chaman. I have spoken to them, they say it has not reached yet.)

Jajje: Yaar is tareh na kar tu... (Hey, don't do this.)

Irfaan: Jhooth nahin bol raha Jajje, sada roza hai. (I am not lying Jajje, I am fasting.)

Jajje: Afjosh da ki hoya yaar? (What happened to Afjosh?)

Irfaan: Afjosh nikal gaya hai, release *ho gaya hai, tusi ...* (Afjosh is out, he's been released, you ...)

Jajje: Kitthe pahunchi hun? (Where has he reached?)

Irfaan: Vo Karachi de kareeb kareeb hai. (He's very close to Karachi.)

Jajje: Tu zara Mansoor nu phone *karke keh de mainu* phone *kar, jeda maal pahunche mainu* phone *kare.* (You call Mansoor and tell him to call me as soon as the consignment arrives.)

Irfaan: Hun Eid di chhuttiyan aa gayee hain na... (Actually there are Eid holidays ...)

Jajje: Kadon? (When?)

Irfaan: Kal se chaar din band hosi. (Four days after tomorrow.)

Jajje: Theek hai, te Mangalwar nu Mansoor nu phone *karin.* (OK, so you call Mansoor on Tuesday.)

Irfaan: Haan, Mangalwar main keh dewanga to tainu bata denga tafseel se. (OK, I will tell him on Tuesday to call you and tell you everything in detail.)

Jajje: Haan, ki maal jaise hi aawe na, mainu phone *kare. main* instruction *de dewanga kis tarah ravana karna hai.* (Yes, that

[186]

he should call me as soon as the consignment arrives, I will give instructions about how it has to be forwarded.)

Irfaan: Theek hai, theek hai, Khuda Hafiz. (OK, OK, God bless.)

It could possibly have remained the biggest mystery in all of hijacking dramas: where did the hijackers disappear?

Pakistani officials denied the five men had come into their country, and promised that they would be arrested if they did. Pakistani intelligence officials also claimed in published reports that the hijackers and the freed prisoners split up and that the hijackers went in the direction of Afghanistan's Herat region, to slip across the border into Iran and eventually find safe haven in a Gulf country. To travel to Herat, the hijackers would have to travel nearly a thousand kilometres to the northwest across hostile mountainous terrain unpopulated for long stretches. Angry officials in Iran also denied the reports. "Rumours are being spread about the presence of the hijackers in Iran in an attempt to deceive the public," government spokesman Hamid Reza Asifi said on 5 January.

Maulana Masood Azhar himself gave a version very different from that of the Pakistani intelligence.

In the first of his several public speeches, the maulana said repeatedly that the hijackers told him immediately after driving off from the Kandahar airport: "*Aap humein nahin jaante, hum kabhi nahin mile*" (You do not know us. We have never met). Azhar was perhaps not aware — or his audience was not aware — of what Taliban Foreign Minister Muttawakil had told journalists of several international news agencies on 25 December after a face-to face-meeting with Chief and another hijacker: The chief hijacker identified himself as Ibrahim, brother of Maulana Masood

Azhar. Realising the crucial implication of this statement only much later, Muttawakil did a turnaround towards the end of the hijacking and said he did not know who the hijackers were.

Surprisingly, his colleague in New York, Maulana Huqeem Mujahid, said something else on 9 January — that "some" of the hijackers were Pakistanis and they had gone to Pakistan. "It is not exactly known where they are headed, but since no other country wants them, the only guess is that they are headed towards Pakistan," Mujahid was quoted as saying in published reports. He said that after consultations between the governments of India and Afghanistan, the UN and the International Committee of the Red Cross in Kandahar, it was realised that no other country would want to give refuge to the hijackers. Mujahid said he did not think the hijackers had officially asked to be "sent" to Pakistan.

"Since some of them are Pakistani, one can guess that they would go to Pakistan," he added.

Nevertheless, Masood Azhar gave the following account of his interaction with the hijackers: The hijackers wept and embraced the militants but would not take off their face coverings or fully identify themselves. "The hijackers said, 'You don't know us. We have never met. We are from India and we respect you and admire you, but we cannot take off our masks,' " Azhar said. As the vehicle headed towards Pakistan, the hijackers remained with Azhar and his two companions for twenty-five minutes, and parted company before crossing the Afghanistan border. However, the hijackers and the released militants were seen driving away from the Kandahar airport in two separate vehicles. According to Azhar's account, at one point the hijackers stopped the vehicle, got out and got into another vehicle, and freed their Taliban hostage, the younger brother of Kandahar Corps Commander Usmani. The hijackers said they were returning to India but not with Azhar, he claimed. Then they were gone.

But Pakistan's government came up with a more incredible story. At a press briefing on 28 December, Foreign Office spokesman Tariq Altaf said the hijacking was a plot of the Indian intelligence agency Research and Analysis Wing. He named an official of the agency who purportedly was masterminding the operation from inside the plane. An Internet web site, www.ummah.net, often called the hub of Islamic thinking in cyberspace, said the hijacking was an attempt by Indian intelligence to malign the Kashmiri freedom struggle by the guerillas. But this theory did not explain why the allegedly Indian-government-backed hijackers would fly out of the country to risk being killed in a storming in Lahore or the UAE or Afghanistan. They could better malign the Kashmiri movement from a domestic airport, with the complete backing of the government.

The truth was different. According to available information from both sides of the border, by the second week of January, the hijackers were secure in a Pakistani intelligence camp called Hamza near the northern town of Rawalpindi. Information was not available after that. According to Indian officials, the hijackers were being protected by Pakistan's Inter Services Intelligence.

Pakistan's Interior Minister Moinuddin Haider told journalists on 1 January: "Pakistan is on high alert, and in case (the hijackers) enter Pakistani territory, they will be apprehended and tried (according to) established international rules." But officials did the opposite. This conversation on Eid day between a Pakistani government official who is addressed by the name Wasi, and a Pakistani diplomat in Washington, shows government complicity in shielding the hijackers when they reached Pakistan after Kandahar.

Voice X: Eid mubarak ho Wasi Sahab, kahiye. Ek second hold *karna.* (Happy Eid, Mr. Wasi. Hold on a minute.)

Wasi: Sir *Eid mubarak aapko bhi ho* Sir. *Kaise hain* sir? *Aap ke mutalik chime goinya* (inaudible) *ho rahi hain?* (Sir, Happy Eid to you as well, Sir. How are you, Sir?)

Voice X: Aap ko terrorist state *declare karein to kab karein, abhi karein ya baad mein karein?* (laughs) (If we declare you a terrorist state, when should we do it? Now or later? [laughs].)

Wasi: Haan? Pakke pakke? Bilkul? (Yes? Sure? Are you certain?)

Voice X: Bilkul ho rahi hai, aap ki harkatein hi aisee hain to kya karein? (It's certainly going to happen. When your activities are like this, what can we do?)

Wasi: Bach sakte hain, jaan chhura kar bhag jayen to bach sakte hain aur kya hai in choron se. (We can escape this, we can run away and save our lives from these thieves, what else?)

Voice X: O bhai, jo inko bithaya hua hai in bandon ko aapne, inko pakden, kisi ko marein ya kisi ko latkayein ya kisi ko saza den, kisi ko kuchch karein to jaan chhutegi varna to nahin chhutati. Yahi, jo aapne bithaya hua hain log jo hain, mukhtalif organisation hain, mukhtalif bande hain ... (O brother, these men you are keeping with you, catch them, thrash one of them, or hang one of them or punish one of them, do something to either of them, only then you will be spared otherwise you've had it. These people you have sheltered, there are different organisations, different men ...)

Wasi: Mukhtalif? (Different?)

[190]

Voice X: Haan, aur kya? Maulana Saheb jo hain ab unko aapne ijazat jo de di, vo lambi chauri takreerein karein to phir zahir hai aap ko terrorist to declare karenge voh. (Yes, what else? Now you have given permission to the maulana to make long speeches, then it's obvious they'll declare you terrorists.) *Wasi: Haan, sahi baat hai. Unko pakar ke puchho to, kam se kam ek din ke liye to pakro.* (Yes, it's true. Catch them and question them, at least detain them for one day.)

Voice X: America ne to kal kaha, aap investigation karein, yeh kya bakwaas kar rahe hain, aur unhone to warning de di hai ki agar kisi American ko nuksaan pahuncha inki takreeron ki vajah se to Pak zimmedar hoga. (America has said yesterday, you launch an investigation, what trash is he talking, and they have given a warning that if any American is harmed because of his speeches then Pakistan will be responsible.) *Wasi: Yeh to ho raha hai. Aap sunayen kaise chal raha hai.* (Yes, this is happening. What about you? How is it going?) *Voice X: Theek hai, bus badmashi kar rahein hain aur kya.* (It's fine, we're upto our tricks, what else?) *Wasi: Jab tak vo bada badmaash aapko aa kar theek na kare then aap karte rahein badmashi.* (Until the big bully comes and sets you straight, you can do all the tricks you like.) *Voice X: Achcha to bus phir, theek hai, aap unhin ko de dein. Aap* (laughs) *chhorein, vo khud hi tiya pancha kar denge barabar. Mullahon ko agar aapne hand over kar dena hai, to karein, phir aap kya beech mein kar rahein hain apna?* (Well, then, it's fine, you hand them over to them only. Leave it to them, they will sort them out themselves. And if you have to hand them over to the mullahs, then you do that. What are you doing in between?) *Wasi: O bhai, vo ataturk kidhar gaya? Vo jo aapke vahan aaya tha ek bade* message *le ke* (laughs) *kyon, aane ke pehle hi unka inteqaal ho gaya kya?* (O brother, where is that Big Turk? The one who came to your place with the big message [laughs]. Did he pass away before reaching?)

Voice X: Achcha bus to phir, theek hai. Phir aapki pitayi hogi, aap tayyar ho jayein, aur kya. (OK, then, it's all right. You are going to be thrashed, so get ready.)

Wasi: Allah ka shukar hai. aapka koi chakkar nahin lag raha? February *mein* programme *hai aane ka?* (God bless. Aren't you coming this side? Is there any programme in February?)

Voice X: Haan, farvaree tak programme hai, *dekhein aur koi gadbad na hui to. Theek hai, to aur achcha, khuda hafiz.* (Yes, there is a programme in February, if nothing else goes wrong. OK then, God bless.)

The Idgaah ground at Bahawalpur was filling up every minute. Thousands of men and children streamed in, most in bright new clothes and caps, several with small scarves slung on their shoulders. Maulana Masood Azhar, the famous son of Bahawalpur, was going to make his first speech in the small town hours after returning home from the Jammu jail. Wearing a shalwar kameez and a chequered scarf, Azhar drove to the ground, where a small wooden bed had been placed and covered with a thin mattress for him to sit. He was encircled by hefty guards from the Harkat-ul Mujahideen wearing camouflage-coloured clothes and carrying Kalashnikovs.

Azhar's fiery speech made it clear why he had been able to get thousands of young men to enlist for his militant group, raise hundreds of thousands of dollars in donations and come to gain his stature. Four days earlier, he had vowed to free Kashmir and attack American interests. His speeches were all fire. After every few sentences, the crowd screamed: "Allah-u-Akbar!" and "Hindustan Murdabad!" Like on other days, there was no one to restrain him today:

he threatened to storm India with half a million mujahideen. He vowed to devastate Indian cities in ways that the Indian authorities could not think of. He incited thousands of common people — even children — to take up weapons against India and to take weapons training. He threatened to make Kashmir a cremation ground where Hindus would be burnt.

"Hamne bahut zulm-o-sitam seh liya. Mussalmano main Allah ko gawah maan kar kehta hoon ... jis Allah ke haath mein ye aasman hai, jiske haath mein ye zameen hai, vo Allah hamara hai vo in qafiron ka nahin hai Allah iman walon ka maula hai. Qafiron ka koi maula nahin. Oh tumne atom bomb banaya hain magar navi ka har unmadi tumhare atom bomb *se zyada taqatbar hai. Tumne* hydrogen bomb *banaye hain, hamara to ek ek baghi hi tumhare* hydrogen bomb *se zyada takatwar hai. Isliye ki tum maut se darte ho hum maut se larte hain. Tum maut se ghabraṭe ho hum maut ko chahte hain. Tumhe maut kadwi lagtee hai, Khuda ki qasam hamein maut shahad se bhi meethi lagtee hai."*

(Translation: We have tolerated enough oppression. O Muslims, I say this and Allah is my witness ... that Allah who holds this sky, who holds this earth, that Allah is ours, it does not belong to these qafirs [non-believers]. Allah belongs to those who have faith. Qafirs have no God. You [India] have made the atom bomb but each of my passionate men is more powerful than that atom bomb. You have made the hydrogen bomb, but each rebel is stronger than your hydrogen bomb. This is because you are scared of death; we fight death. You are wary of death, we are in love with death. Death is bitter to you, but by God, death seems sweeter to us than honey).

Hindustan walon tumhe bata dena chahta hoon ki roz roz Pakistan ko jung ki dhamkiyan dena band kar do. Allah ne mujhe yahan bhej diya hai agar tumne hamare watan-e-azeez ki taraf

*tirchhi nigahon se dekha, main sabse pehle apne saath paanch
laakh mujahedeen lekar* Indian *mein daakhil ho jaoonga aur iske
liye kareeb pure mulk ka daura kar raha hoon Insha' Allah. Paanch
lakh to ifudahee hadaf hain aur poore mulk se mujhe jo paigamat
mil rahe hain mere paas poore mulk se paanch laakh se zyada
mujahedeen Alhumdidullah maujood hain. Meri maaein apne
bachche mujhe de rahee hain ki inko mohal bin Qasim banana,
inhein kisi angrez ka pujari nahin bana. Mere behne apne bhai
mere hawale karke keh rahee hain ki inhe maidan-e-Islam ka Ghazi
banana. Mere poore buzurg mujhe keh rahe hain ki hamari
dadhiyan safed ho chuki hain lekin hun aaj bhi apne haath mein
bandook leke jaane ke liye tayyar hain.*

(Translation: Indians! Let me warn you not to make
threats against Pakistan every day. Allah has sent me here,
and if you cast an evil eye towards my beloved country, I
will first of all enter India with 500,000 of my mujahideen.
This is why I am touring almost the whole nation these
days, so help me God. Half a million are ready, and according to the messages I am getting from across the country,
I have many more mujahideen than these. The mothers are
giving me their sons and asking me to make them followers
of God, not devotees of the Westerners. The sisters are
handing me their brothers and asking me to convert them
into warriors of Islam. The elders are telling me that our
beards are white but even today we are ready to take up
guns and come with you.)

Yeh Hindustan wale apne atom bomb *par guroor mat karna,
apni fauj par guroor mat karna. Hamari fauj bhi bahut taqatwar
hai lekin hamara bachcha bachcha atom bomb hai. Hamara
bachcha bachcha larne ke liye tayyar hai. Agar* Advani *ne ya kisi
aur ne ye buzdili ki aur* Pakistan *ki taraf tedhi nigahon se dekha,
rab-e-kahafa ki qasam main apne mujahideenon ke saath India ke*

shehron mein ghuskar wahan wo kuchch karoonga jo tumhare babu guman mein bhi nahin hai.

(Translation: The Indians should not be too arrogant about their atom bomb, they should not be too proud of their army. Even our army is very powerful but more than that, each child of Pakistan is an atom bomb. Each child is ready to fight. If [Home Minister Lal Krishna] Advani or anyone else tries to be foolhardy and casts a bad eye on Pakistan, by the Almighty, I will sneak into India's cities with my mujahideen and do all that over there, my friends, which you can't even dream about).

Azhar also slammed the Pakistanis and its citizens, saying they were too frightened to take up jehad on a large scale.

Mere gale par khanjar chala diya gaya, aur ye Pakistan *wale jo* Kashmir *ko apni suharat kehte hain, jo* Kashmir *ko apna hissa mante hain door baithe rahe mastiyon mein note jama karte rahe, apne bachchon ko palte rahe. Qufr ko apne gharon mein daakhil karte rahe. Aaj batao to sahi in qafiron ne hamein kya diya hai. Inhone hamare gharon se imaan nikalkar bahar phenk diya. Inhone hamare gharon se Qur'an nikalkar bahar phenk diya. Aaj hamein tabaah karte hain hamare gharon se* football *khelte hain. Aaj duniya ke kitne momalik hain jahan jahan* report *sikwe nigafta hai magar hamein training lene se bhi dar lagta hai, ki kaheen hum par koi dhabba na lag jaye. Ik aam janwar ko bhi apne tahfuz ki fiqr hoti hai magar Musalman ko na apne imaan kee fikar hai na deen ki fikar hai. Jehad mein jakar maut nahin aati. Agar jehad mein maut aani hoti to main aapke saamne na baitha hota. Na* Afghanistan *mein Roos kee goliyan hi mujhe waqt se pehle maar sakin, na unki intezamian ki bambari mujhe halaq kar saki, na* India *ki jailon mein chheh saal tak unke tamam forces milkar mujhe khatam kar saki.*

[195]

(Translation: I bore the crucifix, and these Pakistani [officials] who call Kashmir their territory, who call Kashmir a part of our country, just watched happily and kept bringing up their children and filling up their pockets with money. They welcomed vice into their houses. Tell me what have these qafirs given us? They have thrown out faith from our houses. They have thrown out the Qur'an from our houses. They are destroying us today and playing football with our homes. We are scared of even going for [arms] training, we are scared that it will leave slurs on us. Even common animals are anxious about their protection but Muslims are concerned neither about their integrity nor their religion. No one is killed in jehad. If people were killed in jehad, I would not have been sitting before you. Neither Russian firing could kill me in Afghanistan, nor their bombardment, and neither could Indian forces finish me while they kept me behind bars for six years.)

Afsos hota hai jab Kargil *mein yahan laraee ho rahee thi poora* Hindustan Pakistan *ke khilaaf tayyar ho chuka tha. Hindu baniye ko larne ka tareeqa to ata nahin hai, lekin tijoriyan khol khol kar vo paisa de rahe the. Jabki* Pakistan *ka Musalman jehad ka naam lene se darta hai. Kahin koi mujhe gair mohbal aadmi na kehde. Ye jehad wahi hai jo izzat ki mashaal hai lekin is jehad ko chhoo lene ke baad hum duniyan mein zaleel ho chhuke hain. Is Eidgaah mein Musalmaanon ko ek daawat deta hoon aur qafiron ko bhi ek baat batata hoon. Hum poore* Kashmir *ko vo shamshaan ghat bana denge jahan Hinduon ki tamam lashon aur chitaon ko jalakar raakh kar denge.*

(Translation: It is a shame that when there was a war going on in Kargil, the whole of India was ready to fight against Pakistan. Hindu traders don't know how to fight, but they had thrown open their vaults and were showering money. But the Muslims in Pakistan are scared of taking the name of jehad. It might give them a bad name. This jehad is the torch of valour but after we held it we have been humiliated in the society. I want to give an invitation to Muslims from this Idgaah and I want to tell the qafirs one thing. We will turn the whole of Kashmir into a cremation ground where we will burn the funeral pyres of Hindus to ashes.)

Poora Hindustan ikkiswin sadee ke aane ka jashan mana raha tha, unki agenciyaan keh rahi thin ikkiswin sadi mein hum Pakistan *ko bhi le lenge harap kar lenge. Magar ikkiswin sadee ke aakhri din ikattees disambar unnes sau ninyanabe ko* India *ko badtareen shikast hui jab itni bari fauj ke bawajood unhe mujhe riha karna para. Aur apne jahaaz mein bithakar apne wazeere kharza ke saath mujhe* Kandahar *ke* airport *par lakar mujhe wahan chhorna para. Ikattees tareekh ka ye paigham* India *ko yaad rahega. Insha'Allah vo din door nahin jab too haath jor kar humse kahega ki apna* Kashmir *apne paas wapas le lo.*

(Translation: The whole of India was celebrating the arrival of the twenty-first century, its agencies were claiming that we will seize Pakistan in the twenty-first century. But on the last day of the twentieth century, on the 31st of December, India faced a horrible defeat when, despite their huge army, they had to release me. They had to put me on their plane and bring me to the Kandahar airport with their foreign minister to free me. India will remember the message of the 31st of December. God willing that day is not far when India will beg us and say, please take back your Kashmir).

The speech ended, and the bodyguards brandishing Kalashnikov rifles whisked Azhar into a truck and drove away.

But Azhar could not continue his campaign as planned. He was brandishing too many threats to India and the US.

His remarks had provoked harsh comments from the US government. As the conversation between the Pakistani official in Washington and Wasi in Pakistan showed, Islamabad was realising the need to be seen as taking some symbolic step against the maulana. As Azhar himself said in a magazine interview: "The media coverage of this hijacking put a lot of pressure on the (Pakistani) government, and it wants us to keep a low profile." Weeks later, the maulana was put under "detention," shortly after he publicly launched a new terrorist group.

In Muzaffarabad, capital of Pakistan-controlled Kashmir, Zargar was receiving a huge welcome from his supporters. According to the *Dawn* newspaper, banners were strung across the city with slogans in Urdu and English welcoming Zargar, and describing him as one of the founding members of the ongoing militancy in Kashmir. As Zargar got down from a car, hundreds of members of the Al Umar organisation and the residents of the Narul neighbourhood, where its office is located, rushed towards him to embrace and touch him.

In Kandahar, one man had made a silent return. Saudi billionaire Osama Bin Laden had come back to Kandahar after the hijacking. According to *The Frontier Post* newspaper of Peshawar, Bin Laden had left Kandahar for an undisclosed destination within Afghanistan soon after the hijacked plane landed there. The newspaper said Taliban officials had asked Bin Laden to leave for a safer place because of the large presence of diplomats and journalists during the crisis — and added that Bin Laden's aides feared the hijacking was a drama staged to locate and arrest him.

Kavita Sharma woke up startled and sweating in her residence in New Delhi's Kalkaji neighbourhood. The former hostage, who was on board the hijacked plane, had had that dream again that was haunting her for days since she returned. Burger had shot her in the abdomen. She woke up feeling a searing pain in her abdomen, it refused to go away for long. Sleeping close to her, her husband Vishal was having another nightmare that had refused to go away for days. He saw everything vividly: all the hostages were released, they were walking out happily from the plane, embracing each other, and then suddenly a gunbattle broke out at the Kandahar airport. There was heavy fighting, Vishal ran for cover and suddenly he was shot — in the neck, right in the middle.

The eight-day horror had left the hostages with deep psychological scars. Some cared to show them, others struggled with them on their own. The most prominent signs were common. They started having nightmares, the five who had kept them captive in the most inhuman circumstances haunted them frequently, and they developed small fears. Many became suspicious of people and their frequent questions, many withdrew into their selves, others developed a fear of flying. When asked if he was going to be out of town for some days, a passenger who was counted among the brave ones said: "No comment." Along with their fears, the extraordinary experience would transform the passengers in many ways — above all, they would realise the worth of morsels of food and bottles of water and a clean toilet and the freedom to stretch one's legs.

But the crew members did not have the time to assess their fears and depressions. Within days of returning home, Capt. Sharan, Capt. Rajinder, Flight Engineer Jaggia, Senior Flight Purser Anil Sharma and the rest of the crew was back at work. They would not fly to Kathmandu for some time, as Indian Airlines had shut down all flights to Nepal. But for months, each time the cockpit door opened they would be uneasy, when a passenger suddenly got up they would probably get startled, and monkey caps — wherever they saw them, in parks, streets or the marketplace — would ignite an old memory.

Weeks later, the hijacked Airbus was ready to fly again, after being done up in Bombay with new carpets and rubber mats. Four damaged seats that had been soiled with blood were replaced. For days, the stink inside the plane did not go away.

Maulana Masood Azhar, now happily married, was missed in India by his former jail inmates. But someone else was still looking for him. Magistrate Bala Jyoti walked into her court on 6 January and wanted to know why Azhar, who was facing trial in the attempted jailbreak case, had not been brought to the courtroom. Chanchal Singh, the superintendent of the Kot Bhalwal jail, had sent her a letter saying the accused could not be presented before the court. "This letter is without any reasonable excuse," the magistrate said. It took another hearing and an apology to explain to the magistrate that all cases against Azhar had been withdrawn. He had been released from the jail without any judicial order.

In Nepal, Gajendra Man Tamrakar was back nursing his pride. He had been falsely painted as a hijacker and no one had apologised to him. But Tamrakar realised within days that his hostage status was bringing him unexpected gains and could actually prop up his sagging career as a television comedian. He had become a celebrity.

But another man in Lucknow city was about to suffer because of his similarity to a notorious celebrity: it was Vakil Ahmed's misfortune that he looked a lot like Burger.

The police swooped down on him on 8 January as he stood at the Amausi airport waiting for a relative to fly in from New Delhi. A telephone call from an alert citizen had set police jeeps racing across the town to Ahmed's house, his office and then the airport, from where the police thought he was about to get away. A mole on his cheek — which did not come off — saved Ahmed. Burger did not have one.

On the same day, an acquaintance of the hijackers was calling a house in Islamabad where some relatives of Allah Baksh's family live.

Voice X: Salam A'laikum ji, yeh Islamabad *ka number hai?* (Hi, is this an Islamabad number?)

Voice Y: Ji. (It is.)

Voice X: Main Haleema ki behen hoon, England *se baat kar rahi hoon. Hor sab kaise hain?* (I am Haleema's sister calling from England. How's everybody?)

Voice Y: Ji salam A'laikum, sab theek hain. (Everyone is fine.)

Voice X: Salauddin, Tariq, sab bachche keh rahe hain hum baat karenge Haleema baaji se. Vo keh rahe hain Munji ko Eid mubarak. Bol Rayatullah kaisa hai? Rayatullah to bol ki kabhi khat likha kar, kabhi phone kiya kar, yeh to bahut bada aadmi ban gaya hai. Kahan hai voh hain, kahan? (Salauddin, Tariq, all the children are saying we will talk to Haleema auntie. They are saying Happy Eid to Munji. Tell me, how is Rayatullah? Tell him to write to me sometime, or call me, he's become a very big man. Where is he?)

(Inaudible)

Masood Azhar azad ho gaya hai, bolo baaji ne bahut bahut mubarik boli hai. Hor usko bolna ki vo jahaz ki vo hijacker mein tu shamil tha, mujhe pata hai. Bola han Maulvi Sahab bahut khush hue. Keh rahe the meri taraf se mubarak usko bol ek jo hai vo.

[201]

(Masood Azhar has been freed, tell him auntie has said congratulations. And tell him that he was involved in the hijacking of that plane, I know that. Tell him Maulvi [priest] was very happy. He was saying say my congratulations to him, what's his name?)

Mera khayal mein hijacker mein ek jo hai vo Farooqui hai. Kahin pakda nahin jae? (Laughs) *Usko (Rayatullah) bolna hai ki baaji ne bahut mubarak boli hai, Eid ki bhi, hor Masood Azhar ke azad hone ki bhi.*

(I think one of the hijackers was Farooqui. I hope he is not caught. [Laughs] Tell him auntie has sent her many congratulations — for Eid as well as for the release of Masood Azhar.)

Away from the world of the happy survivors, a young woman slept a heavy sedated sleep in her desolate house. Doctors had thrown a hazy curtain between Rachna Katyal and her agony, but she would often wake up from the slumber and rip away the curtain of forgetfulness, cry for hours and let herself be lulled to sleep.)

Rachna Katyal had not taken off her colourful bridal bangles.